Popular Mechanics

WEATHERPROOFING & INSULATION

Albert Jackson and David Day

Hearst Books
A Division of Sterling Publishing Co., Inc.
New York

Popular Mechanics
Steve Willson, U.S. Project Editor
Tom Klenck, U.S. Art Director

Created, edited, and designed by Inklink
Concept, editorial, design and art direction: Simon Jennings
Text: Albert Jackson and David Day
Design: Alan Marshall
Illustrations: David Day, Robin Harris, Brian Craker, Michael Parr, Brian Sayers
Photographs: Paul Chave, Peter Higgins, Simon Jennings, Albert Jackson

Hearst Books
Project editor: Joseph Gonzalez
Cover design: Celia Fuller

Library of Congress Cataloging-in-Publication Data available.

10 9 8 7 6 5 4 3 2 1

Published by Hearst Books
A Division of Sterling Publishing Co., Inc.
387 Park Avenue South, New York, NY 10016

Popular Mechanics and Hearst Books are registered trademarks of Hearst Communications, Inc.

www.popularmechanics.com

For information about custom editions, special sales, premium and corporate purchases, please contact Sterling Special Sales Department at 800-805-5489 or specialsales@sterlingpub.com.

Distributed in Canada by Sterling Publishing
c/o Canadian Manda Group, 165 Dufferin Street
Toronto, Ontario, Canada M6K 3H6

ISBN-13: 978-1-58816-534-3
ISBN-10: 1-58816-534-5

Contents

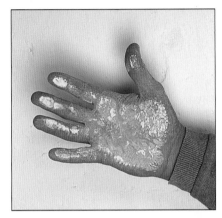

Moisture problems

Moisture problems and the dampness they cause can be detrimental to your health and to the condition of your home. So try to locate and eliminate any sources of moisture as quickly as possible, before wet or dry rot develops. There are three major types of moisture problems: penetrating moisture from external leaks, rising moisture from osmosis through basement floors, and condensation moisture that's generated inside the house.

Penetrating moisture

Penetrating moisture is the result of water entering the structure from outside. This is usually considered the most damaging type of moisture problem and therefore the one that worries homeowners the most. The obvious symptoms, like water dripping from a ceiling, collecting below the front door, or running down the inside of windows, occur only during wet weather. And they dry out after a couple of dry days, sometimes leaving only subtle stains behind.

Isolated damage suggests that water has entered only at a single point. With a little methodical investigation, you should be able to locate the source accurately. But general dampness and humidity indicate a larger overall problem, one that may be hard for a non-professional to diagnose. Roof leaks are notorious for being difficult to trace.

Obvious problems like worn out weatherstripping, defective caulk, and a few missing roof shingles aren't hard to fix. To diagnose and solve more complicated problems, it's a good idea to call in a contractor.

Principal causes of penetrating moisture
1 Broken gutter
2 Leaking downspout
3 Missing shingles
4 Damaged flashing
5 Faulty pointing
6 Porous bricks
7 Cracked masonry
8 Cracked stucco
9 Loose shingles
10 Defective seals around frames
11 Missing weatherstripping

Rising moisture

Rising moisture is caused by water from the ground soaking through basement walls and floors. Most newer houses have concrete foundations and floors with impervious vapor barriers installed when they were being built. These barriers are designed to eliminate, or at least greatly reduce, the amount of moisture passing through. But they are only as good as the product used and the installation methods employed. Too often these barriers are treated almost as an after thought.

In many older homes, especially those with stone foundations and dirt or gravel floors, there are no barriers to water penetration, to say nothing of any vapor barriers in place. The amount of rising moisture entering these structures can be very high. During wet weather it's not uncommon to have water pouring through the walls and floor. This is why so many old houses have big sump pumps. With no barriers in place, moisture is a constant problem, even during dry spells. The weather may be dry outside, but the soil around the house is always damp.

PENETRATING MOISTURE: PRINCIPAL CAUSES

CAUSE	SYMPTOMS	REMEDY
Broken or blocked gutter Rainwater overflows, typically at the joints of old gutters, and saturates the wall directly below, preventing it from drying out normally.	Damp patches appearing near the ceiling in upstairs rooms, and mold growth immediately behind the leak.	Clear leaves and silt from the gutters. Repair the damaged gutters or replace with new gutters.
Broken or blocked downspouts A downspout that has cracked or rusted through soaks the wall behind the leak. Leaves get lodged at the break and plug the entire spout.	An isolated patch of wet, often appearing halfway up the wall. Mold growth behind the downspout.	Clear the blockage and repair or replace the cracked or corroded downspout. Paint wall with stain blocker primer and repaint.
Loose or broken roof shingles Defective shingles allow rainwater to penetrate the roof.	Damp patches appearing on upstairs ceilings, during a heavy downpour.	Replace the faulty shingles and repair any damage underneath.
Damaged flashing The joint between any section of the roof and a side wall of the house, and the roof areas around chimneys, plumbing stacks and roof vents are sealed with flashing. Flashing is usually made of aluminum or occasionally copper. If the flashing breaks or is torn, water draining off the roof will enter the building behind or below it.	Wet patches on the ceiling extending from the wall toward the roof ridge, or around a chimney or a roof vent. Damp patch on the side wall near the walls junction with an adjoining roof. Water dripping from an exhaust fan in the bathroom.	If the existing flashing appears to be intact, cover the leaking area with plastic roof cement. If it is damaged, replace it, using similar material.
Faulty pointing Aging mortar between bricks in an exterior wall or chimney is likely to crack or fall out; water is then able to penetrate to the inside of the wall.	Isolated damp patches or sometimes widespread patches on walls and near chimneys, depending on the extent of the deterioration.	Repoint the joints between bricks, then treat the entire wall with a water-repellent coating.
Porous bricks Bricks in good condition are weatherproof, but old soft bricks become porous. As a result, the wall behind the problem bricks becomes saturated, particularly on the side of the house or chimney that faces prevailing winds and therefore most of the driving rain.	Widespread dampness on the inside of exterior walls. A noticeable increase in dampness during a downpour. Mold growth appearing on walls and ceilings.	Repair or replace faulty bricks and coat the area with a clear water-repellent sealer.
Cracked brickwork Cracks in a brick wall allow rainwater (or water from a leak) to seep through to the inside wall.	An isolated damp patch on the inside wall of the house directly behind the crack.	Replace any damaged bricks and mortar, and cover with a clear water-repellent sealer.
Defective stucco Cracked or damaged stucco encourages rainwater to seep between the stucco and the wall sheathing underneath. The water can't evaporate before it's absorbed by the wall.	An isolated damp patch, which may become widespread. The trouble can persist for a day or two after rain stops.	Fill small cracks with stucco repair and reinforce the crack. Remove and replace extensively damaged sections. Then paint the whole area with exterior paint.
Damaged coping If the coping stones (on some brick houses) are missing or the joints are open, water can penetrate the wall.	Damp patches on ceiling below or near where the coping stones are located.	Install new stones in fresh mortar or replace the mortar between sound stones.

Dampness: causes and cures

PENETRATING MOISTURE: PRINCIPAL CAUSES

CAUSE	SYMPTOMS	REMEDY
Blocked drip groove Exterior window sills should have a groove running along the underside of the sill from one end to the other. When rain runs under the sill, the water falls off at the groove. If the groove is full of paint, water will go over it and into the wall.	Damp patches along the underside of a window frame. Rotting wood sills on the inside and outside. Mold growth appearing on the inside face of the wall below the window.	Clean out the drip groove. Then coat the sill with wood preservative and repaint.
Failed caulk around windows and doorframes Wood trim around windows and doors often shrinks, causing the caulk to crack and let in rain water.	Rotting woodwork and patches of damp around windows and doors.	Repair the trim and seal the gap between the trim and siding with silicone caulk.
No weatherstripping Weatherstripping around and under doors should keep out rain water. When it's worn or missing, water can easily enter.	Damp floorboards just inside the door. Rotting along or next to the door threshold.	Replace old weatherstripping around door. Repair threshold with epoxy filler, coat with preservative, and paint.
Bridged wall cavity Mortar inadvertently dropped onto a wall tie connecting the inner and outer leaves of a cavity wall allows water to bridge the gap.	An isolated patch of damp appearing anywhere on the wall, particularly after a heavy downpour.	Open up the wall and remove the mortar bridge, then waterproof the wall externally with paint or clear repellent.

RISING MOISTURE: PRINCIPAL CAUSES

CAUSE	SYMPTOMS	REMEDY
Stone foundation walls If a house has a stone foundation, water and moisture can enter through any spaces between the stones or cracks in the mortar.	Standing water or very high humidity in the basement. Mildew or rot on the floor framing members above.	Excavate the perimeter of foundation wall and parge with a heavy layer of mortar. Install a sump pump and dehumidifier.
Dirt or gravel floor Water and water vapor evaporates into basement air from the soil.	Wet or damp floor. Mildew or rot on the floor framing members above.	Pour reinforced concrete floor or install a sump pump and dehumidifier.
No sump pump A sump pump removes standing water from basement floors after floods or long periods of rain have saturated soil surrounding the foundation.	Standing water in your basement.	Install a sump pump and dehumidifier.
Severely cracked concrete floor Superficial cracks are of no concern, but deep cracks that go though the floor into the soil below let ground water into the basement.	Standing water on the floor or damp areas next to the crack. Worse during very wet weather.	Fill the cracks with hydraulic cement.
Severely cracked concrete wall Cracks in solid concrete or concrete block walls that go through the wall allow water from the surrounding soil to enter.	Water stains on the wall and standing water on the floor below the crack.	Make sure the gutters and foundation perimeter drain system are working properly. Then fill cracks with hydraulic cement.

Remedies for curing different moisture problems are suggested in the charts on the previous pages. Below are key repair techniques.

Waterproofing walls

Waterproofing foundations walls is the sort of thing that is best done when a house is being built, not years later.

Foundation walls work best when they are made of solid concrete or concrete block and mortar. Both types need extensive waterproofing added to the outside of the wall and a complete perimeter drainage system installed before the foundation is backfilled with soil. If the waterproofing or drainage fail, the only certain way to make the repairs is to excavate around the walls and replace the waterproofing and drainage.

Providing a drip molding

Because water cannot flow uphill, a drip groove on the underside of an external window sill forces rainwater to drip to the ground before it reaches the wall behind (**1**). When painting the house, scrape out all the old paint from drip grooves so a bridge cannot form (**2**). If an external window sill does not have a precut drip groove, it's

Sealing around window frames

Scrape out the old or loose caulk from around window and door trim and fill the cracks with silicone caulk. Run the tip of the caulk tube along the edge of the trim to get a smooth even bead. If the gap is too wide to be filled with one bead, fill it with a second after the first has dried.

To fill especially deep gaps, first

Bridged cavity

A bridged cavity is sometimes a problem in brick veneer houses. When bricks are being laid, mortar occasionally drops behind the bricks into the cavity between the house wall and the brick veneer wall. When this dropped mortar hits and sticks to wall ties, it can collect moisture that is between the walls and sometimes transfer it through the inner wall and stain the room wall.

The easiest way to deal with the problem is to coat the outside of the brick

Exterior walls are easier to treat, because in most cases this just means repainting them and caulking all the gaps between the siding boards and the siding and trim. In the worst cases, where the siding has remained unpainted for so long that the wood is split, cracked and coming loose from its fasteners, the siding has to be replaced. If you replace it with wood siding, make sure that all boards are back primed before they're installed. Then apply two top coats of high quality paint.

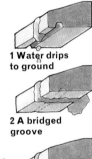

1 Water drips to ground

2 A bridged groove

3 Drip molding

worth adding a drip molding underneath. Just glue and nail a ¼ inch square strip about 1½ inches from the front edge of the sill (**3**). Paint or stain the drip molding to match the sill.

spray a layer of expanding foam filler into the crack. Let it dry according to the manufacturer's instructions. Then finish filling the gap with caulk.

Fill gaps around window and door trim with silicone caulk

with a water repellent sealer. This should reduce the amount of moisture between the walls and thus the amount of moisture leaking into the house.

Bridged cavity results from mortar being dropped on wall ties

Air carries moisture in the form of water vapor. Its capacity to carry depends on its temperature. As air becomes warmer, it absorbs more water, something like a sponge. When water-laden air comes into contact with a surface that is colder, the air cools until it can no longer hold the water it has absorbed. The water condenses and is deposited, in liquid form, on the cold surface.

Conditions for condensation

A great deal of moisture vapor is produced by cooking and by using baths and showers, and even by breathing. The air in a house is normally warm enough to hold the moisture without reaching its saturation point—but in cold weather the low temperature outside cools the external walls and windows below the temperature of the heated air inside. When this happens, the moisture in the air condenses and runs down windowpanes and soaks into the window trim and wall surface below. Matters are made worse in the winter when windows and doors are kept closed, so that fresh air is unable to replace humid air before it condenses.

The root cause of condensation is rarely simple because it is usually the result of a combination of air temperature, thermal insulation, humidity and poor ventilation. Tackling just one of these problems in isolation may exaggerate the symptoms or transfer the condensation elsewhere. The chart on the facing page lists major factors and some common remedies.

Condensation usually appears first on cold glass.

Condensation: causes and cures

CONDENSATION: PRINCIPAL CAUSES

CAUSE	SYMPTOMS	REMEDY
Insufficient heat In cold weather the air in an unheated room may become saturated with moisture.	General condensation.	Heat the room to increase the ability of the air to absorb moisture without condensing.
Kerosene heaters This type of heater produces as much water vapor as the fuel it burns, causing condensation to form on cold windows, exterior walls and ceilings.	General condensation in rooms where the heater is used.	Substitute another form of heating.
Uninsulated ceilings Moist air readily condenses on cold ceilings.	Widespread damp and mold. Lines of ceiling joists are clear because mold doesn't grow as well along the joists, which are relatively warm.	Install attic insulation.
Uninsulated walls Moist air condenses on cold walls.	Damp patches or mold, particularly around the window casings.	Install wall insulation and/or storm windows.
Uninsulated pipes Cold-water pipes attract condensation. The problem is often wrongly identified as a leak in the pipe.	A line of dampness on a ceiling following the path of a pipe. An isolated wet spot on a ceiling where water drops from a pipe. Beads of moisture on the underside of a pipe.	Insulate your cold-water pipes with plastic foam tubes.
Cold windows When exterior temperatures are low, windows usually show condensation before other features do. The glass is thin, so it cools quickly and stays cold until it warms up outside.	Foggy windowpanes and water collecting in pools at the bottom of the glass.	Reduce moisture in the room and/or install storm windows.
Sealed fireplace If a fireplace opening is blocked up, the air trapped inside the flue cannot circulate and therefore condenses on the inside and eventually leaks.	Damp patches appearing anywhere on the chimney, the firebox or the hearth.	Ventilate the chimney by inserting a grille through the area that's blocked.
Attic insulation blocking vents If attic insulation blocks soffit or roof vents, air cannot circulate properly and condensation appears on rafters and roof sheathing.	Widespread mold or rafters, attic floor joists and the underside of roof sheathing.	Unblock the vents and install a roof fan if necessary.
Condensation after remodeling If you've done work that involved new mortar or plaster, condensation may be the result of these materials expelling a lot of moisture as they dry out.	General condensation affecting walls, ceilings, windows and floors.	Wait for the new work to dry out, then review the situation.

Damp basement

Being below ground level, the walls and floors of a basement invariably suffer from dampness to some extent. The best way to solve serious moisture problems is from outside by installing new waterproofing on the walls and a new perimeter drainage system. But this can be very expensive. For this reason, minor moisture problems usually are solved from the inside as described below. To improve the chances that interior treatment will work, check the following: all gutters and downspouts should be working properly, the soil around the foundation should be graded away from the house, the basement should be sufficiently ventilated and well heated, and a room dehumidifier should be installed.

Treating the floor

New concrete floors should always have a vapor barrier installed. But many old ones don't have one, or it isn't working properly. To create a surface barrier, you can seal the floor with a heavy-duty, moisture curing polyurethane.

To prepare the floor, make sure it's clean and grease free. It might take several washings to get it clean, but good preparation is time well spent. The bond between the polyurethane and the floor will be much stronger as a result.

Then fill any cracks and small holes by first priming these areas with one coat of polyurethane. One hour later fill the crack and holes with a mortar made from six parts sand, one part cement, and enough polyurethane to produce a stiff paste. Fill deep cracks carefully, making sure to push the mortar all the way into the cracks with the edge of your trowel. Smooth the surface of the mortar so it's flush with the surrounding area.

Let the mortar cure and do your best to dry out the entire floor. The polyurethane can work in damp conditions but it will penetrate a dry floor better. Use a wide floor brush to apply the first coat. Do not exceed the coverage recommendations printed on the container. After two or three hours, apply a second coat, wait for it to dry, then follow up with a third and a fourth coat, with proper drying in between. After three days curing time, the floor should be ready for use.

Treating a wall with bitumen-latex emulsion
1 Skim coat of mortar
2 Bitumen latex coating
3 Dry sand layer
4 Plaster

Treating a floor with moisture-curing polyurethane
Cover the floor with three or four coats of polyurethane.

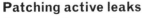

Patching active leaks

You can patch any cracks that are actively leaking water, using quick-drying hydraulic cement. Sold in powder form, you just mix it with water and it expands as it hardens, sealing out the moisture. To apply it, first undercut the crack using a cold chisel and hammer. Mix some cement and hold it in a gloved hand until it's warm, then push it into the crack. Hold it in place with your hand for a couple of minutes, until it is hard.

Moisture-curing polyurethane can be used to seal the walls of a basement as well as the floor. If want to paint the walls, do so within 24 hours after treatment to achieve maximum adhesion. After the first coat of paint is dry, you can add another coat of paint at any time.

Bitumen-latex emulsion

If you plan to plaster the basement walls, you can seal out modest moisture by using a relatively cheap bitumen-latex emulsion. This is sometimes used in a concrete floor as a waterproofing agent and as a waterproof adhesive for some tiles and parquet flooring. But it isn't suitable as an unprotected covering, for either walls or floors.

If old plaster is in place, remove it and repair the wall underneath with a skim coat of mortar to create a smooth surface. Once the mortar is cured, paint the wall with two coats of the bitumen emulsion. Before the second coat dries, embed some clean, dry sand into the emulsion to provide a key for the plaster.

Polyethylene barriers

If you want to use drywall to finish the basement walls instead of plaster, you should still prepare the walls as described above. But once the bitumen emulsion has cured, install furring strips, to receive the drywall, on the foundation walls. These can be nailed in place with masonry nails or attached with self-tapping concrete screws. In most cases, attaching the furring on 24-inch centers is the accepted approach.

This is a good time to consider adding rigid polystyrene foam insulation to the walls. It's easy to work with (just press it between the furring strips), impervious to moisture, and affordable. The improved R-value of your basement walls will make the living space much more comfortable and it will cost less to heat. Different thicknesses are available. Choose the best one for you and match the thickness of the furring strips to the thickness of the insulation.

After the furring strips (and insulation) are in place, install a continuous polyethylene sheet vapor barrier against the furring. Staple it in place and make sure to tape all the seams. Then install the drywall panels and finish the joints with tape and joint compound. Prime the surface and paint it.

Wet rot and dry rot | Treating rot

Rot can occur in unprotected lumber inside your house, and in buildings and fences outside that are subject to moisture or high levels of water vapor. Damp conditions allow fungal spores to develop and multiply, eventually destroying the lumber. Severe fungal attack can cause serious damage and requires immediate attention. The two most common types are wet rot and dry rot.

Recognizing rot

Signs of fungal attack are easy enough to detect—but some strains are more damaging than others, and so it is important to be able to identify them.

White furry deposits or black spots on lumber, drywall or wallpaper are mold growths. Usually, these are the result of condensation. When they are wiped or scraped off, the structure shows no sign of physical damage except some staining. Eliminate the source of the condensation. Then, treat the moldy area by washing it with a fungicide solution or a mixture of 16 parts warm water and one part household bleach.

Wet rot

Wet rot only occurs in lumber that has a high moisture content. Once the cause of the moisture is eliminated, further deterioration is stopped. Wet rot often attacks the framework of doors and windows that have been neglected, allowing rainwater to penetrate the joints and adjacent lumber. The first sign is often peeling paint. Removing the paint will reveal wood that is spongy when wet, but dark brown and crumbly when dry. In advanced stages the grain splits, and thin dark-brown fungal strands will be evident. Always treat wet rot as soon as you find it.

Dry rot

Once it's established, dry rot can be an extremely serious form of decay. It attacks wood that has a much lower moisture content than wood that's attacked with wet rot. Dry rot occurs in badly ventilated and confined indoor spaces, unlike wet rot, which usually thrives outdoors.

Dry rot exhibits different characteristics depending on the extent of its development. It spreads by sending out fine pale-gray strands in all directions (even through masonry) to infect drier lumber. It will even pull water from damp wood. Dry rot can progress at an alarming rate. In damp conditions these strands are accompanied by white growths resembling cotton wool, known as mycelium.

Over time, dry rot develops wrinkled pancake-shaped bodies. These produce rust-colored spores, and when expelled, the spores cover surrounding lumber and masonry. Infested wood becomes brown and brittle, with cracks across and along the grain, causing it to break up into cube-like pieces. You may detect a strong, musty, mushroom-like smell, produced by the fungus.

Wet rot

Dry rot spores

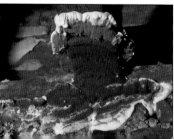

Dealing with wet rot

Once you have eliminated the cause of the moisture, cut away and replace any damaged wood. Then paint the repaired areas and the surrounding woodwork with three heavy coats of fungicidal wood preservative. Brush the liquid into all the joints and end grain.

Then apply a wood hardener to reinforce the damaged wood and fill any voids with epoxy wood filler. Finish up by priming and painting.

Coat damaged wood with hardener

Dealing with dry rot

Unless the outbreak is minor and self-contained, dry rot should be treated by a professional who specializes in this work. Because this fungus is able to penetrate masonry as well as wood, figuring out just how far it has spread can be very difficult.

If you do decide to treat small areas yourself, begin by eliminating any sources of dampness. And make sure there is adequate ventilation to prevent the rot from returning. Cut out all infected lumber to at least 18 inches beyond the last visible sign of rot. Wire brush any infected masonry. Then, collect all the debris in plastic bags and burn it.

Use a liquid fungicidal preservative to kill any remaining spores. Apply three generous coats to all woodwork, masonry, and plaster or drywall within five feet of the infected area. You can also spray on three coats of the preservative. Just be sure to wear any and all protective clothing recommended by the manufacturer.

If you have a wall that has been penetrated by strands of dry rot, drill regularly spaced staggered holes into it from both sides. Angle the holes downwards, so the fluid will collect in them and saturate the wall internally. Repair the holes after you've completed the treatment.

Coat all replacement wood with preservative, and if possible, immerse the end grain in a bucket of preservative for five to ten minutes. Once the preservative is dry, prime and paint the affected areas.

Preventive treatment

Because fungal attack can be so damaging, it is well worth taking precautions to prevent it. Regularly paint and maintain door and window frames, where water is able to penetrate easily. Seal around them, and fill any cracks in the siding with caulk. Provide adequate ventilation in all areas, especially the attic and basement. Eliminate any sources of moisture, such as leaks from plumbing pipes, the roof, and foundation walls.

Looking after lumber

Any lumber that's used outside or in high moisture areas inside the house, should be treated with wood preservative. Brush or spray at least two coats on all boards, paying particular attention to joints and end grain.

Immersing lumber

Any lumber that will be in contact with the ground, especially fence posts, needs to be treated with preservative. Either buy treated lumber for the job, or do the treating yourself. Fence posts can be coated on the outside by simply brushing on preservative. But the end of the post that will go in the ground should be immersed in a bucket of perservative to protect the end grain of the wood. Keep each post in the bucket for at least 10 minutes.

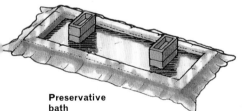

Preservative bath

You'll get the best results, however, if you totally immerse the posts in a preservative bath. To do this, fabricate a tub by stacking up loose bricks for the walls and lining the depression with a thick sheet of polyethylene. Fill the trough with preservative and immerse the posts, holding them down with bricks to prevent them from floating. Leave them in the preservative overnight.

Wood preservatives

There are many different chemical preservatives on the market, designed for specific uses outside and inside the house. Be sure you choose the correct one for the job at hand.

Liquid preservatives For treatment of existing indoor and outdoor wood, choose a liquid preservative that you can apply with a brush. Although all wood preservatives are toxic, if you follow the manufacturer's instructions for proper use, they can be used safely.

Common preservatives are zinc and copper napthenate, and trubutylin oxide (TBTO). Traditional creosote and pentachlorophenol (penta) are no longer sold for consumer use. These chemicals are carcinogens and are highly toxic.

Liquid preservatives are sold in hardware stores, lumber yards and home centers. Some are also sold in paint stores. When buying preservatives make sure you get a preservative, not a water repellent. Preservatives carry antifungal chemicals that penetrate the wood. Repellents are exterior coatings that simply protect the outside of the wood against water damage. Some preservatives are paintable, others are not. And some come with stains incorporated into their formulation to color the wood.

Clear   Wood Colored   Green

Pressure-treated lumber Pressure-treated lumber is the best choice for any new outdoor construction where the wood will come in contact with the ground or concrete. Decks and fences are the two most common examples.

Usually this lumber is rated for two different applications: ground contact and above-ground use. Inhaling the treatment chemicals can be harmful. So wear a dust mask when sawing and don't burn scraps.

Safety with preservatives

All preservatives are flammable—so don't smoke while you are using them, and extinguish any open flames. Wear protective gloves and goggles when applying preservatives. And wear a face mask respirator when using them indoors. Provide good ventilation while working, and don't sleep in a freshly treated room for 48 hours to allow time for the fumes to dissipate completely. Immediately wash off any preservative from your skin. If some splashes in your eyes, flush them with water immediately and get medical help right away.

Windows: types and construction

● **Window frames**
Most frames and sashes are made up from molded sections of solid wood. However, mild steel, aluminum, and rigid plastic are also used.

1 Casement window

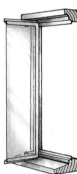

2 Glazing bars

3 Steel casement

The purpose of any window is to allow natural light into the house and to provide ventilation. Traditionally, windows were referred to as "lights," and the term "fixed light" is still used to describe a window or part of a window that doesn't open. The part of a window that opens is called a sash. The sash can slide up and down or side to side in tracks or can be hinged on the side or the top. Windows with side-hinged sashes are usually called casement windows. Window sashes can also pivot, and a group of smaller glass panes can be operated together to form a jalousie window.

Most window frames and sashes are made of solid wood. In many cases, the outside surfaces are clad with painted aluminum or colored vinyl.

Casement windows

One of the more common windows is the simple hinged or casement window. Traditional versions are made of wood, and are fabricated much like doors. Vertical side jambs are joined to a head jamb at the top and a sill at the bottom (see below). Depending on the size of the window, the frame is sometimes divided vertically by a mullion with another side-hinged casement on the other side, or horizontally by a transom **(1, left)** and an awning window.

A side-hung casement sash is attached with either a continuous hinge or with butt hinges. A lever handle, sometimes called a "cockspur," is mounted on the sash stile and is used for opening, closing, and locking the sash. A casement stay attached to the bottom rail holds the sash open in various positions. With a top-hung casement (or awning sash), the stay also secures the window in the closed position.

Glazing bars, lightweight, molded strips of wood, steel, or vinyl, are often used to divide the glazed areas of a window into smaller panes **(2)**.

Mild-steel casement windows **(3)** have relatively slim welded frames and sashes. They are strong and durable, but will rust unless protected by galvanized plating or high-quality metal paint. Modern versions are galvanized by a hot-dip process, then finished with a colored polyester coating.

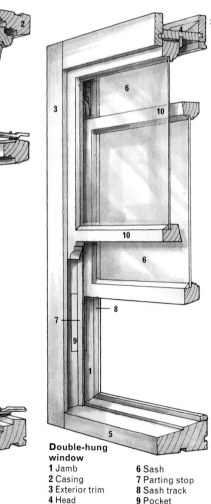

Casement window
1 Jamb
2 Head
3 Sill
4 Casement sash
5 Awning (vent) sash

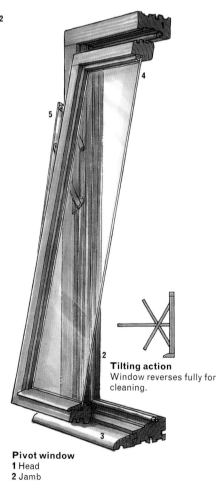

Tilting action
Window reverses fully for cleaning.

Double-hung window
1 Jamb
2 Casing
3 Exterior trim
4 Head
5 Sill
6 Sash
7 Parting stop
8 Sash track
9 Pocket
10 Meeting rail

Pivot window
1 Head
2 Jamb
3 Sill
4 Sash
5 Pivot hardware

Double-hung windows

Vertically sliding windows are usually known as double-hung windows. In this design, both the top and the bottom sash can be opened.

Traditional wooden sash windows (see opposite) are constructed with a box frame in which the jambs are composed of three boards, joined together at the top corners. The side jambs are joined to the sill at the bottom. Windows are sized to fit standard wall thicknesses. When installed, the inside edge of the jambs should be flush with the wall surface and ready for casings to be nailed in place. For thicker walls, extension jambs are nailed to the window jambs to bring them flush with the wall.

If the window has counterweights, they're installed behind the side jambs, with access provided by a small removable piece of the jamb, called a pocket.

The sashes of a double-hung window are held in tracks formed in the side jambs. They are separated by a parting stop. The top sash slides in the outer track and overlaps the bottom sash at horizontal meeting rails. The closing faces of the meeting rails are beveled. This bevel makes the sashes wedge together when closed, which prevents the sashes from rattling. This also allows both rails to separate easily as the window is opened. The sashes are locked by hardware that joins them when closed.

Pivot windows

Wood-frame pivot windows (see opposite) are constructed in a similar way to casement windows. But their special hinge mechanism allows the sash to be rotated so that both sides of the glass can be cleaned from inside. Using the built-in safety catch, the sash can be locked when open or when fully reversed.

Similar pivoting windows, usually called roof windows, are made for pitched roofs. These windows are usually double-glazed and some come with blinds built into the window. The window is usually protected on the outside by an aluminum cladding, and a flashing kit provides a weatherproof seal between the window and the roof.

Jalousie windows

A jalousie window is a specialized pivot window. The panes are unframed strips of glass, typically ¼ inch thick, that are capped at each end by plastic or aluminum carriers. These carriers pivot on channels screwed to the window frame. The panes are linked by a mechanism that allows them to be opened or closed simultaneously. The exposed edges of the glass are ground and polished.

Jalousie windows provide excellent ventilation and light transmission, but unfortunately offer minimal security unless outfitted with specialized locks.

Aluminum windows

Aluminum window frames are installed in new houses, and often are used as replacement windows for old wood or steel units. The aluminum is extruded into complex sections to hold double-glazed sashes. Finished in several colors—usually white, silver, black, brown, and bronze—aluminum window frames require no maintenance.

They are sold, like wood windows, in many different standard sizes with many different features. They are manufactured in complete units ready for installation. To reduce water damage from condensation, hollow sections of the metal frame incorporate an insulating material to create a thermal break.

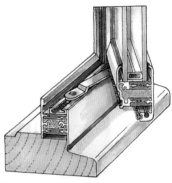

Extruded-aluminum window in a wooden frame

Vinyl windows

Rigid vinyl windows are similar to aluminum ones. They are typically manufactured in white plastic and, once installed, require only minimal maintenance.

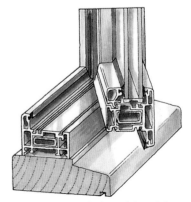

Extruded-plastic window with metal reinforcing

Wood casement— exterior

Wood casement— interior

Metal casements

Vinyl casements

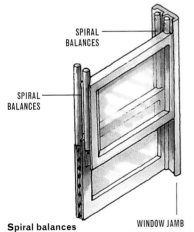

SPIRAL BALANCES

SPIRAL BALANCES

Spiral balances
WINDOW JAMB
The exposed balances are set into grooves in the side jambs of the window. Modern wooden, aluminum, and vinyl sashes have spring-assisted spiral balances.

Use two sets of panes for wide opening.

Repairing a broken window | Installing new glass

Glazing putty
Traditional linseed-oil putty is made for glazing wood frames. It dries slowly and is hard when set. All-purpose putty for wood and steel frames has similar properties. Both putties tend to crack if they are not protected with paint. Newer acrylic-based glazing putty is an all-purpose type that is easy to use and dries quickly, ready for painting.

Even when no glass is missing, a cracked windowpane is a safety hazard and a security risk, and no longer provides a weatherproof barrier to the elements. It should be replaced promptly.

Temporary repairs For temporary protection from the weather, tape a sheet of polyethylene over the outside of the window frame until you can replace the glass. If the window is merely cracked, it can be repaired temporarily using a clear self-adhesive waterproof tape. Applied to the outside, this tape gives an almost invisible repair.

Safety with glass Unless the window is at ground level, it's safer to remove the sash in order to replace broken glass. However, a fixed window has to be repaired on the spot, wherever it is. Large pieces of glass should be handled by two people. Don't work in windy weather, and wear gloves and protective goggles when removing glass.

Repairing glass in wood frames
In wood window frames, the glass is set into a rabbet cut in the frame, and then bedded in putty. Small wedge-shaped fasteners, known as points, are also used to hold the glass in place. Traditionally, linseed-oil putty was used for glazing wood frames. However, acrylic-based glazing putty, which is fast drying and durable, can be used instead. In some cases a wood glass bead is screwed to the rabbet to hold the pane.

Removing the glass If the glass has shattered, leaving jagged pieces set in the putty, grip each piece separately and try to work it loose **(1)**. It's best to start working from the top of the frame. Old putty that is dry will usually break away easily. But if it won't, cut it out, using a utility knife or a glazier's knife and a hammer **(2)**.

Work along the rabbet to remove the putty and glass. Pull out the points with pliers **(3)**.

If the glass is merely cracked, run a glass cutter around the perimeter of the pane, about 1 inch from the frame, to score the glass **(4)**. Apply strips of tape across the cracks and scored lines, then tap each piece of glass until it breaks free and is held only by the tape **(5)**. Carefully remove individual pieces of glass, working from the center of the pane.

Once all the glass and points are removed, completely clean out the remnants of old putty from the rabbets. Seal the wood with primer. Measure the height and width of the opening to the inside of the rabbets, and have your new glass cut ⅛ inch smaller in height and width to provide some room for adjustment.

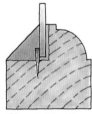

Glass held with putty

Glass held with bead
Some wood frames feature a wood beading, embedded in putty and screwed to the frame. Unscrew the beading and scrape out the putty. Install new glass in fresh putty and replace the beading.

1 Work broken glass loose

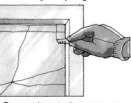

2 Cut away old putty

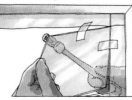

3 Pull out old points

4 Score glass before removing cracked pane

5 Tap glass to break it free

Purchase new glazing points and enough glazing compound for the frame. The rule of thumb is that 1 pound of putty will fill an average-sized rabbet about 13 feet long.

Working with putty
Knead a palm-size ball of putty (glazing compound) to an even consistency in your hand. You can soften putty that is too stiff by adding a little linseed oil.

Press a thin, continuous band of putty into the rabbet all around the frame. Smooth it out with a putty knife. Lower the new pane of glass into the bottom rabbet, then press the rest of the pane into place. Apply pressure close to the edges only, squeezing the putty to leave a continuous seal around the whole pane. Secure the glass by installing glazier's points every 8 inches around the pane. Make sure they lay flat with the surface of the glass. Trim the surplus putty from the back of the glass with a putty knife.

Apply more putty to each rabbet on the outside of the glass. Using a putty knife, work the putty to a smooth finish at a 45-degree angle. Make neat miters at the corners. Let the putty set for about three weeks, then paint the frame. The paint should lap the glass slightly to form a weather seal.

1 Install new points

Acrylic glazing putty
Acrylic glazing putty is packaged in a a cartridge and applied with a caulking gun. Run a bead of putty into the rabbet. Bed the glass in place and secure it with glazing points. Then apply a continuous bead of putty all around the frame and smooth it to a 45-degree angle with a putty knife. Allow at least 4 hours for it to cure, then trim off any excess material and clean the glass with water.

Buying glass

Always carry panes of glass on edge to prevent them from bending, and wear heavy work gloves to protect your hands. Also wear goggles to protect your eyes when removing broken glass from a frame. Wrap broken glass in thick layers of newspaper before you dispose of it, to reduce the possibility that the people who pick up the trash will be cut. Or check with a local glass shop; it may be willing to add your glass to its scrap pile to be sent back to the manufacturer for recycling.

Basic glass cutting

It is not usually necessary to cut glass at home because most suppliers are willing to do it for you. But sometimes it's more convenient to cut it yourself. A handheld glass cutter with a steel wheel is inexpensive, easy to use, and can handle most common jobs.

Cutting glass successfully is largely a matter of practice and confidence. If you have not done it before, make a few practice cuts on waste pieces of glass and get used to the feel of the tool before cutting the project piece.

Lay the glass on a flat surface covered with a blanket. (Patterned glass should be placed pattern side down and cut on its smooth side.) Clean the cutting surface with mineral spirits.

Place a T-square at the cutline **(1)**, and check your measurement. If you're working on a small piece of glass or don't have a T-square, mark the glass on opposing edges with a felt-tipped pen and use a straightedge to join the marks and guide the cutter.

Lubricate the cutter wheel by dipping it in light machine oil or kerosene. Hold the cutter between your middle finger and forefinger **(2)** and draw it along the guide with a single continuous stroke. Use firm, even pressure throughout the stroke and run the cutter off the end. Slide the glass over the edge of the table **(3)** and tap the underside of the scored line with the back of the cutter. Wearing gloves, grip the glass on each side of the scored line **(4)** and snap it in two. Or you can place a wood dowel under the length of the cutline and push down evenly on both sides of the pane until the glass snaps.

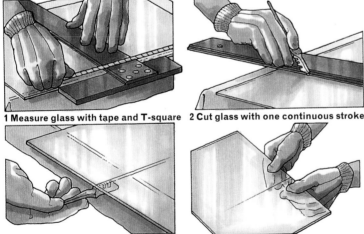

1 Measure glass with tape and T-square

2 Cut glass with one continuous stroke

3 Tap underside to initiate cut

4 Snap glass in two

Cutting off a thin strip of glass

To reduce a slightly oversize pane of glass, remove a thin strip by scoring a line as described above, then gradually remove the waste with nibblers (see far right) or a pair of pliers.

Nibble away thin strip with pliers

Cutting glass

You can buy most types of glass from your local hardware store or home center. Often the salespeople can advise you on the type you need and cut the glass to your specifications. If the piece of glass you want is big, or you want to order a lot of glass, look for a glass supply store in the Yellow Pages. Specialty suppliers have a greater selection of different glasses and will usually deliver.

Glass thickness

Once expressed by weight, the thickness of glass is now measured in inches. If you are replacing old glass, measure its thickness to the nearest 32nd of a inch. If you can't find an exact match, buy a slightly thicker glass for safety.

Although there aren't any strict regulations concerning the thickness of glass, it is advisable to comply with the recommendations set out in the Uniform Building Code. The thickness of glass required depends on the area of the pane, its exposure to wind pressure, and the vulnerability of its location, for example, whether it is next to a play area. Tell your supplier what the glass is needed for to ensure that you get the right type.

Measuring

Measure the height and width of the opening to the inside of the frame rabbet. Check each dimension by taking measurements from at least two points. Also check that the diagonals are the same length. If they differ significantly, indicating that the frame is out of square, make a cardboard template of the opening and take it to the glazier. In any case, deduct ⅛ inch from the height and the width to allow room for adjusting the glass when you install it. When ordering an asymmetrical piece of glass, make an exact template of the piece you need and take this to the supplier.

Glass cutters

Glass nibblers
Use nibblers to trim off the edge of a pane.

● **Acrylic glazing**
Use clear acrylic sheet as an alternative to glass when cutting awkward shapes. Use a fret saw and files to shape acrylic.

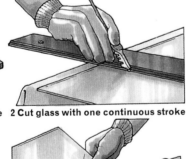

Cutting circles and drilling holes

Cutting a circle in glass

Stick the suction pad of a compass glass cutter on the glass. Then adjust the cutting head to match the radius of the specified hole. Score the circle around the pivot point, applying firm, even pressure as you go. Now score another, smaller, circle inside the first one **(1)**. Remove the cutter and crisscross the inner disc with straight cuts, then make radial cuts about inch apart in the outer rim. Tap the center of the scored area from underneath **(2)**, then remove the pieces of glass. Finally, tap the outer rim and nibble away the waste with pliers.

To cut a disc of glass, scribe a circle with the compass cutter, then score tangential lines from the circle to the edges of the glass **(3)**.

1 Score circles with even pressure

3 Cutting a disc
Scribe the circle, then make tangential cuts from it to the edge of the glass.

Smoothing the edges of cut glass

You can grind down the cut edges of glass to a smooth finish using wet-and-dry abrasive paper wrapped around a wood block. Start with medium-grit paper wrapped tightly around the block. Dip the block, complete with paper, in water and begin by removing the sharp corners along the edge with the block held at 45 degree angle to the edge. Keep the abrasive paper wet. Then sand all the edges flat, using long strokes with the block held flat on the edge. Repeat the process with progressively finer-grit papers. Finally, polish the edge with a wet wooden block coated with pumice powder.

2 Tap center of scored area

Using a glass-cutting template

Semicircular windows and glazed openings above some exterior doors in older homes have segments of glass mounted between radiating bars.

Standard panes may be available for glazing some modern semicircular windows, but if you're doing restoration work on an old house, you may need to cut the glass yourself.

Each piece of glass is a segment of a larger circle. But usually you can't use a compass cutter for the job because the circle is bigger than the capacity of the cutter. You'll need to make cardboard templates to serve as guides for scoring the glass with an ordinary cutter.

Remove the broken glass and clean up the frame. Then tape a sheet of paper over the window and, using a crayon, take a rubbing of the opening **(1)**. Remove the paper pattern and tape it to a sheet of thick cardboard. To provide clearance for fitting between glazing bars, and to allow for the thickness of the glass cutter, make the cardboard template about ⅛ inch smaller than the pattern on all sides.

Use double-sided tape to attach the template to the glass. Score around it with the glass cutter **(2)**, running all cuts to the edge of the glass, and then snap the glass in the usual way.

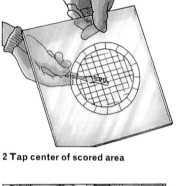

1 Take rubbing of shape with crayon

2 Cut around template, using even pressure

Drilling a hole in glass
Use a brace with special glass-cutting bits.

Drilling a hole in glass

There are special spear-point drill bits for boring holes in glass. You will need to use a handheld bit brace or a power drill set to run at a low speed.

Mark the position for the hole, no closer than 1 inch to the edge of the glass, using a felt-tipped pen. When drilling mirrored glass, mark the back, coated surface.

Place the tip of the drill bit at the center of the mark and, with light pressure, twist it back and forth until it grinds a small recess and no longer skids over the glass. Use glazing putty to form a small ring around the work area, and fill the inner well with kerosene as a lubricant.

Run the drill at a steady speed and light pressure, since too much pressure may break the glass. When the tip of the bit emerges, turn over the glass and drill from the other side. Drilling straight through from one side risks chipping out the back surface.

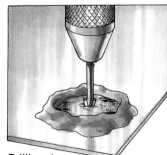

Drilling glass
Always run drill in lubricant to reduce friction

Circle compass cutter

Leaded glass windows

Leaded-glass windows are glazed with small pieces of glass joined by strips of lead, known as cames. In many windows, the cames form a lattice that holds rectangular or diamond-shaped panes of clear glass. But in other windows, particularly stained-glass units, the structure is free-form and incorporates colored and textured glass.

Supporting leaded panes

Leaded panes are relatively weak and can sag with age. If you have an old window that is bowing, you can support it with a ¼-inch steel rod.

Drill a ¼-inch hole on each side of the window frame, placing the holes about halfway up the sides, in line with a horizontal piece of came if possible. Drill one hole twice as deep as the other. Flatten the window carefully with the palm of a gloved hand, or use a board to spread the load. Solder a few short lengths of copper wire to the back of the came in line with the planned location of the support rod.

The length of the rod should equal the distance across the inside of the window frame, plus twice the depth of the shallow hole drilled in the frame. Locate the rod in the holes, inserting it in the deeper hole first.

Twist the soldered wires around the rod so that the window is tied to it. Finish the rod with black paint and, if necessary, form a waterproof seal on both sides of the window by pushing glazing compound into the cames.

Replacing broken glass in leaded windows

It is always easier to replace a piece of glass with the window out of its frame. But because leaded windows are fragile, it's sometimes safer to carry out the repair with the window still in place. If the complete unit does have to be removed, carefully chip out the glazing putty and support the whole panel against a board as it is taken out.

Cut the cames around the broken pane at each joint, using a sharp knife **(1)**. If possible, make the cuts on the inside of the window.

With a putty knife, lift the edges of the cames and pry up the lead until it is at right angles to the surface of the glass **(2)**. Lift or tap out the broken pieces and scrape away any old putty. If you are working with the leaded panel in place, support it from behind with your gloved hand or with a board attached to the back side of the window frame.

Make a paper template of the shape and size of the replacement glass you need. Then lay this template on the new glass and trace around it. Make the cuts with a glass cutter and a straightedge, keeping the cut just to the inside of the line **(3)**. Try the glass for fit and, if necessary, sand down problem spots with wet-and-dry paper.

Mix some black polish (available from glass suppliers) into a ball of ordinary glazing putty and apply a thin bead to the open cames. Then bed the glass into the cames with even pressure. Fold over the edges of the cames to secure the glass. Rub the cames smooth with a piece of wood.

Thoroughly clean the cut joints in the cames with fine steel wool and resolder them **(4)**, using an electric soldering iron and resin-core solder.

Use your thumbs to press colored putty under the edges of the cames on the inside of the window. Run a pointed dowel against the cames to remove excess putty. Remove any smeared putty from the glass with a rag dampened with mineral spirits.

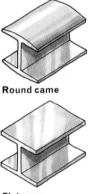

Came styles

Round came

Flat came

Beaded came

Twisted-wire tie

Support sagging leaded glass with a metal rod.

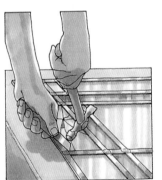

1 Cut cames with sharp knife

2 Pry lead up with putty knife

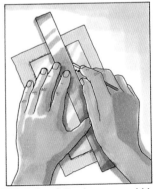

3 Cut glass following paper rubbing

4 Resolder joint after installing glass

Double-glazed units

Sticking and rattling windows

Installing stepped glazing

Some double-glazed window units are designed with a step built into the edge. This provides a positive surface for the unit to bear against. These panes are installed much like regular panels, but a resilient packing piece is added to support the extra weight.

Stepped units
Follow this sequence when installing double-glazed, stepped units.
1 Set the resilient packing in glazing compound.
2 Install the double-glazed unit and secure with glazing points.
3 Fill the rabbet with glazing putty.

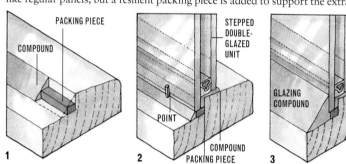

Installing square-edged units

Square-edged units are sealed with butyl glazing compound and held in place with beading. For the conventional method shown here, you will need glazing compound, glazing blocks, and beading nails (see below).

Apply two coats of primer or clear sealer to the rabbets in the frame and let dry. Lay a bed of the nonsetting butyl glazing compound in the rabbets. To keep the glass from moving in the compound, place packing blocks on the bottom rabbet and the spacer blocks against the back of the rabbet. Set the spacers about 2 inches from the corners

and about 12 inches apart. Locate the spacers behind the points where the beading will be screwed in place.

Set the double-glazed unit into the rabbet and press it firmly in place. Apply an outer layer of compound and place another set of spacers against the glass, positioned to match the spacers installed behind the glass.

Press each bead into the compound and against the spacers. Screw the beading strips in place with brass or galvanized screws. Remove excess compound and clean the glass. Prime and paint as needed.

Using beading.
Set square-edged units in butyl compound.
1 Set the packing and spacers in compound.
2 Install the unit, apply more compound, and place spacers behind the beading screw locations.
3 Press the beading against the spacers and attach with screws.

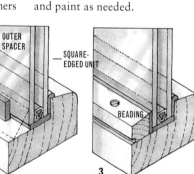

Glazing metal-framed windows

Steel window frames are made with galvanized sections that form a rabbet for the glass. These windows are glazed the same way as a wood-framed window, using general-purpose glazing compound or acrylic glazing putty. The glass is secured in the frame with spring clips (see right), set in holes in the frame and covered with putty. To replace the glass in a metal frame, follow the sequence for

wood frames but use clips instead of points. Before installing the glass, remove any rust and apply a high-quality metal primer.

Modern aluminum and plastic double-glazed frames use a dry glazing system that features synthetic rubber gaskets. These are factory installed and should be maintenance free. To repair a broken pane, consult the manufacturer.

The sashes of wood casement windows tend to swell and stick in wet weather. Once they dry out, they should work properly and you should take the time to prime and paint them. This will reduce or totally eliminate the swelling because the water won't reach the wood.

Curing sticking windows

If a casement window sticks persistently in all weather, it may be due to paint buildup. To repair, strip the old paint from the edges of the sash and the rabbets in the frame. Then prime and paint these surfaces.

If a window has been painted shut, free it by working a utility-knife blade between the sash and the frame. Sand the edges smooth until the sash closes properly, remove any dust, then prime and paint the sanded edges. The same repair advice pertains to all window sashes that have been painted shut.

Curing rattling windows

The rattling of a casement window is usually caused by a poorly installed lever lock. If the lever handle is worn, you can either replace it with a new one or adjust the position of the old one so it works better.

Old double-hung wood windows are notorious for rattling. The most common cause is a sash (usually the bottom one) that fits too loosely in its tracks. To repair it, remove and replace the stop, or glue a thin strip to the side of the stop, to create a narrower track. Rub candle wax on both sliding surfaces if the repair is a little too tight.

If the top sash is rattling, shim it out in a similar way and adjust the lock's position to pull the sashes together.

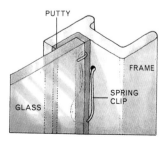

Repairing rotten frames

Old wood windows have always deteriorated to some extent. But regular maintenance and prompt repairs can restore them so they work properly for many years to come. New frames and those that have been stripped of their old finish should be treated with a wood preservative before you paint them.

Regular maintenance The bottom rail of a wood sash is particularly vulnerable to rot, especially if it is left unpainted. Rainwater seeps in behind old glazing putty, and moisture is gradually absorbed through cracked or flaking paint. Carry out an annual check and deal with any faults. Cut out old putty that has shrunk away from the glass and replace it. Remove flaking paint, repair any cracks in the wood with wood filler, prime, and repaint. Don't forget to paint the bottom edge of the sash.

Replacing a sash rail

Where the rot is so severe that the sash rail is beyond repair, cut it out and replace it. This should be done before the rot spreads to the stiles, otherwise you will eventually have to replace the whole sash frame. Start by removing the sash from the window frame.

It is possible to make the repair without removing the glass, though it is safer to remove it if the window is large. For either approach, you'll need to cut away the putty from the damaged rail.

Usually, the bottom rail is tenoned into the stiles **(1)**. To remove the rail, saw down the joint shoulder lines from both sides of the sash **(2)**.

Make a new sash rail and cut it to length so a full-width tenon is at each end. Position the tenons to line up with the mortises in the stiles. Cut the shoulders of the tenons to match the rabbeted sections of the stiles **(3)**. If there is a decorative molding on the stile, cut it away to leave a flat shoulder **(4)**. Cut slots in the ends of the stiles to receive the new tenons.

Glue the new rail securely into place with a waterproof glue and reinforce the two joints with pairs of ¼-inch hardwood dowels. Drill the stopped holes for the dowels from the inside of the frame so they won't break through the outer surface. Stagger the dowels for a stronger joint.

When the adhesive is dry, plane and sand the surface as needed and remove all the dust. Treat the new wood with a clear preservative. Fill the rail rabbet with glazing compound, then prime and paint as soon as the putty is dry.

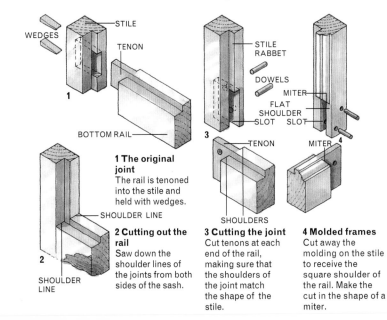

1 The original joint
The rail is tenoned into the stile and held with wedges.

2 Cutting out the rail
Saw down the shoulder lines of the joints from both sides of the sash.

3 Cutting the joint
Cut tenons at each end of the rail, making sure that the shoulders of the joint match the shape of the stile.

4 Molded frames
Cut away the molding on the stile to receive the square shoulder of the rail. Make the cut in the shape of a miter.

Replacing a rail in a fixed window

The frames of some fixed windows are made like sashes but are screwed to the jamb. After the glass has been removed and the frame unscrewed, this type of fixed window can be repaired in the same way as the casement of sash windows (see below left).

First remove the putty and the glass, then saw through the rail at each end, close to the stile. Use a chisel to remove what remains of the rail and to carve the tenons out of the stiles. Cut a new length of rail to fit between the stiles, and cut slots at both ends of the rail to receive the loose tenons **(1)**. Cut these slots so that they line up with the stile mortises, and make each slot twice as long as the depth of the mortise. Cut two loose tenons to fit the slots, and two packing blocks to force the loose tenons into place. These blocks should have one sloping edge **(2)**.

Removing glass.
Removing glass from a window frame in one piece is not easy—so be prepared for it to break. As a precaution, apply adhesive tape across the glass to bind any broken pieces together. Chisel away the putty to leave a clean rabbet, then pull out the points. Steady the glass and lift it out when it's free.

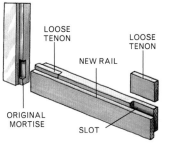

1 Cut slots at each end for loose tenons

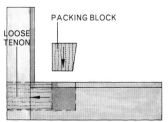

2 Fitting the tenons
Insert the loose tenons, push them sideways into the mortises, and wedge with packing blocks.

Reassembling the frame

Apply an exterior waterproof glue to all of the joining surfaces. Then place the rail between the stiles, insert the loose tenons, and push them sideways into the mortises. Drive the packing blocks behind the tenons to lock them in place. When the adhesive has set, trim the packing blocks flush with the rabbet in the rail. Then treat the new wood with preservative, replace the glass, and add new glazing compound. Repaint once the putty is dry.

Repairing rotten sills

The sill is a fundamental part of a window frame, and because of its size and location, suffers from more exposure to the elements. This exposure can lead to rot. Repairing a sill usually is not a difficult job, but replacing one can be.

A window frame is constructed in much the same way as a doorframe. The head and side jambs are the same width, but the sill is wider and sloped to the outside to shed water. If you just need to repair chips, cracks, and worn depressions, you can work on the sill without removing any window parts. Just choose a day or two when fair weather is forecast. But if you have to replace a wood or stone sill, it's better to remove the window first. If this is impractical, you can replace the sill in place; it's just more difficult.

Replacing a wood sill for a sash window

Ideally, to replace a rotted windowsill you should remove the entire window, carefully disassemble the old sill from the jamb sides, use it as a template, then cut and install a new sill and replace the window. However, sills can be replaced without removing the window, provided you work patiently and have some basic woodworking skills.

Begin by carefully splitting out the old sill. Cut through it crosswise in two places with a saw to remove the middle portion, then

gently pry the end sections away from the jambs. Hacksaw any nails holding the sill to the rest of the frame.

Use a piece of cardboard to make a template for a new sill, shaped to fit between the jambs and beneath the exterior trim. Cut a 10-degree bevel along the upper outside edge of the sill, extending to the inside edge of the sash. Fill the area beneath the sill with insulation, install the sill with 16d finishing nails, then thoroughly fill all the seams with silicone caulk.

Decaying windowsills
Repair deteriorating sills before serious decay sets in.

Repairing a stone subsill

The traditional stone sills featured in older houses may become eroded by the weather if they are not protected with paint. They may also suffer cracking due to subsidence in some part of the wall.

Repair any cracked and eroded surfaces with a quick-setting waterproof cement. To do this, clean any dust or debris from the cracks. Then dampen the stone with clean water and work the cement well into the cracks. Smooth the surface of the patch flush with the surface of the sill.

Depressions caused by erosion should be undercut to provide the cement with a

good hold. A thin layer of cement simply applied to a shallow depression in the surface will not last. Use a cold chisel to cut away the surface of the sill at least 1 inch below the finished level and remove all traces of dust.

Make a wooden form to the shape of the sill and temporarily nail it to the wall. Dampen the stone, pour in the cement until it's level with the top of the form, then smooth it with a trowel. Allow the patch to cure for a couple of days before removing the form.

Casting a new subsill

Cut out the remains of the old stone sill with a hammer and cold chisel. Make a wood form shaped exactly like the old sill. The form must be made upside down, its open top representing the underside of the sill.

Fill two-thirds of the mold with fine aggregate concrete, tamped down well. Then add two lengths of steel reinforcing bar (rebar), in the middle of the concrete, and fill the remainder of the form. Set a piece of ⅜ inch wood dowel into notches previously

cut in the ends of the mold. This is to form a drip groove in the underside of the sill.

Cover the concrete with polyethylene sheeting or dampen it regularly for two or three days to prevent rapid drying. When the concrete is set (allow about seven days), remove it from the form and clean up any rough edges with a cold chisel or handheld power grinder. Reinstall the sill in a bed of mortar, and caulk all joints with silicone caulk.

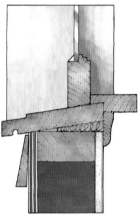

Wood sill on sash window in wood-frame wall

Encase sill in wood form to make repair

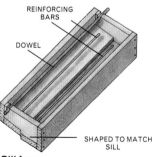

REINFORCING BARS

DOWEL

SHAPED TO MATCH SILL

Sill form

Replacement windows

Lumberyards and home centers offer a wide range of replacement windows in wood, vinyl, and aluminum. Some typical examples are shown below. Unfortunately, the exact window size you need may not be available. You have two options: Order custom-made windows or modify your rough openings to fit a standard replacement-window size.

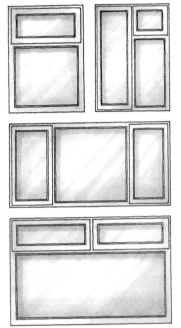

Casement windows

Double-hung windows

Window buying

Most people want to replace their windows because they don't work well mechanically, or because they allow too much heat to escape in winter.

Replacing windows is expensive, so it's tempting to use low-cost units. Unfortunately, these windows don't always solve the problems you're having. It's almost always a better idea to install higher-quality windows. The long-term performance and energy savings are worth the extra cost.

Replacing windows

The style of the windows is an important element in a house's appearance. When replacing windows in an older house, you might find it better, and not necessarily more expensive, to have new windows custom made to fit your openings.

Planning and permits Window replacement doesn't usually require a building permit, unless you live in a historic district that regulates what you can do to the exterior of your house. But if you plan to alter your windows significantly—for example, by permanently removing one or by adding a new window in a new place— call your local building department to see if you need a permit.

All codes have certain minimum requirements, especially for windows on second and third floors. Code authorities want to make sure that at least some windows are big enough for occupants to get out in case of fire. Some localities are also interested in the R-value of the window glazing, in an effort to improve the energy efficiency of the housing stock.

Buying replacement windows As mentioned earlier, replacing windows can be a problem if your window openings do not match standard sizes. You'll either have to alter your openings to fit standard sizes (which can be nearly as expensive as buying the new windows), or you can buy custom-made windows that will fit your openings.

Most contractors who install replacement windows supply the new windows and dispose of the old ones after removal. This is the best way to get the job done, but you should carefully compare contractors and window brands before making your choice.

Replacing casements

Measure the width and height of the window opening. Windows in brick walls will need a wood subframe. If the existing one is in good condition, take your measurements from the inside of this frame. Otherwise, take them from the brick and plan on replacing the frame before installing the new window. Order the replacement window accordingly.

1 Pry out pieces of old frame

Remove the old window by first taking out the sashes. Remove any exposed hardware that may be holding the window frame in the opening. Pry out the frame and cut through any fasteners with a hacksaw or a reciprocating saw. Usually the frame can be pried or driven out of the opening in one piece. But if it's wedged tight for some reason, saw through it in several places and pry the pieces out with a crowbar **(1)**. Clean up the opening.

2 Install new window   3 Drill screw holes

Remove all the protective packaging from the window and slide it into the opening. Check it for level and plumb **(2)** and shim the jambs to keep the unit from moving. Drill screw holes through the jambs into the jack studs or the subframe behind the window jambs **(3)**. Check for level and plumb again, then drive the screws.

Insulate around the window frame, then install any necessary exterior trim and the interior casings. Set all nailheads and cover them with wood filler or caulk. Prime and paint.

Replacing windows

Replacing a window in a brick wall

Bay windows

A bay window is an assembly of smaller windows joined together to yield a big window that projects out from the house wall. The side windows are usually set at one of three angles: 90, 60, or 45 degrees. Curved bays are also available.

The perimeter of a bay window is supported either with brackets of different types or with a shout wall that is part of the wall framing. The bay is protected by a small roof that is attached to the house wall.

Bay windows in brick houses can break away from the main wall because of foundation subsidence. You should hire a contractor for this type of problem. Lesser damage from slight foundation movements can be repaired once the ground has stabilized. Repoint the mortar joints and apply silicone caulk to gaps around the window frame.

Replacement bays Like other windows, old bay windows can be replaced with new ones. But your chances of finding a new bay in just the right size are slight. Usually the opening has to be adjusted, which for bays is complicated by the presence of the roof. Choosing a custom-made bay is probably your best strategy. It may be more expensive, but using something the right size should keep the installation costs to a minimum.

Bow windows

These are windows constructed on a shallow curve, and (like bay windows) they normally project from a flat wall. Complete bow windows are available from window manufacturers, ready for installation. You can use a bow window to replace any type of window, as long as the rough opening is big enough to fit the new window.

To install a bow window, modify the rough opening as needed. Center the bow in the opening, shim it plumb and level, then nail it into place. Install braces beneath the window to support it. And construct a shallow roof over the top to shed rain and snow. Add flashing and new trim where necessary, then caulk all the joints with silicone caulk. Add insulation between the window and the rough opening, then install the interior trim.

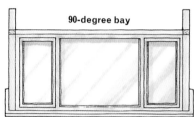
90-degree bay

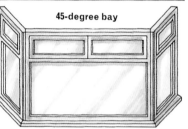
45-degree bay

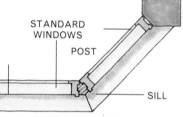
STANDARD WINDOWS

POST

SILL

Standard windows joined to make a bay window

Modern angled bay with decorative lead flashing

Bow window

Window replacement in a brick wall isn't much more difficult than replacing a window in a wood-frame wall. The job is well within the ability of most do-it-yourselfers.

Remove the sashes, then take out the old window frame from inside the room. Pry off the casing, then the window jamb. Cut away the drywall or plaster if necessary. Remove any obvious fasteners holding the frame to the brick, then strike the outside edge of the sill with a heavy hammer and a wood block. When the window frame is free, lift it out of the opening **(1)** and remove any debris left behind.

Lift the new window into the opening and adjust it from front to back so that both side jambs are the same distance from the outside of the brick wall. Check the window frame for level and plumb and wedge the corners of the frame at the top and the sill. If there's space left at the sides between the window and the brick wall, fill the space with bricks and mortar **(2)**. To solidly anchor the window, you can screw metal brackets to the sides of the window frame and set these brackets in mortar joints in the brick wall.

When the mortar is set, replaster the inner wall and replace the casing. Finish up by applying silicone caulk to the joints between the outside bricks and the window frame to keep the weather out.

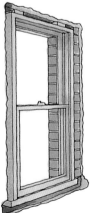
1 Lift out old frame   **2 Fill gaps with brick**

Double-glazed roof windows are becoming increasingly popular for replacing old skylights, especially on attic-conversion jobs. The windows usually come with complete flashing kits that are designed to fit a wide range of different roof pitches.

Roof windows that have center-pivoting sashes can be used on just about all roofs. Because the sash in these windows operates, the window can provide ventilation as well as lots of light. They are relatively easy to install using only common remodeling tools. And most of the work is done from inside the house. Once they are installed, the glass can be cleaned comfortably from the inside. Accessories like blinds and remote-opening devices are also available. Most manufacturers also give you glazing options to reduce heat loss and sun glare.

Roof windows used in a traditional building

Choosing the size

The manufacturers of roof windows offer a wide range of standard sizes.

The installed height of the window should be determined by the pitch of the roof and by how the window will be used. Manufacturers produce charts that give the recommended dimensions depending on the roof pitch. To provide a good view, the bottom rails should not obstruct that view at normal seating height. The top of the window shouldn't cut across the line of sight of someone who is standing.

Generally, this means that the shallower the pitch of the roof, the taller the window needs to be. The top of the window should remain within

Installing a roof window

Start by stripping off the roof-covering materials over the area to be occupied by the window. The final placing of the frame will be determined by the position of the rafters and the roofing. Start by setting the bottom of the window frame at the specified distance above the nearest full course of shingles and try to position it so you'll have half or whole shingles at the sides.

Brace the rafters from inside by installing posts beneath them. Then cut through the roof sheathing and rafters to make the opening, following the dimensions given by the manufacturer. Cut and nail headers and trimmers to the opening (see below) to achieve the correct height and width.

With the glazed sash removed, screw

comfortable reach for accessibility.

Smaller window units can be arranged side by side or one above the other. When deciding on a design, bear in mind how it will look on the outside of the house, not just on the inside.

Though you probably won't need permission to install the window if you're replacing an old unit, code restrictions often apply to any job that requires cutting a new hole through the roof. Check with your building department before beginning work.

The manufacturers of roof windows supply instructions for all types of roofs. Below is a summary of how to install a roof window in an ordinary asphalt shingle roof.

the window frame in place with the brackets provided. Make sure the top of the frame is level, and check that the frame is square by measuring across its diagonals; they should be equal.

Complete the outside work by installing the flashing and new shingles, working up from the bottom of the frame. Replace the sash.

Install insulation between the window frame and the rough opening and replace the insulation in other accessible areas if it was damaged during construction. Install drywall panels to close up the opening around the window and finish all the drywall joints with compound and tape. Add trim to the inside of the window jambs and prime and paint the ceiling.

Window height
The height should enable someone sitting or standing to see out of the window with ease.

Internal blinds are available

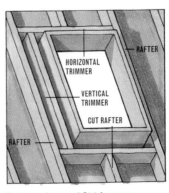

HORIZONTAL TRIMMER

VERTICAL TRIMMER

CUT RAFTER

RAFTER

RAFTER

Cut opening and fit trimmers

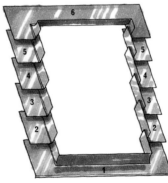

6

5

4

3

2

5

4

3

2

1

Flashing kit showing order of assembly

Doors: types and construction

At first glance, there appears to be a great variety of doors to choose from—but most of the differences are purely stylistic and they are, in fact, all based on a relatively small number of construction methods.

The wide range of styles can sometimes tempt people into buying doors that are inappropriate for the house they live in. When replacing a front door, it's especially important to choose one in keeping with the architectural style of your house.

Buying a door You can buy interior and exterior doors made from softwood or hardwood, the latter usually being reserved for special rooms or entrances where the natural features of the wood can be appreciated. Softwood doors are for more general use and most are intended to be painted. However, some people prefer to apply a clear finish.

Glazed doors are often used for front and rear entrances. Traditionally these feature wood-frame construction, though modern steel doors can be bought in standard sizes, complete with double glazing and numerous accessories.

Frame-and-panel doors are usually supplied in unfinished wood, so you can stain, paint, or clear finish them to suit your taste.

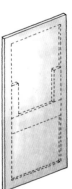

Exterior flush door

Door sizes Doors are made in several standard sizes, which meet most domestic needs. The two most common heights are 6 feet 8 inches and 7 feet. Widths usually start at 2 feet 2 inches and go to about 3 feet in 2-inch increments. Most residential doors are either 1⅜ inches or 1¼ inches thick.

Older houses often have relatively large doors to the main rooms, but modern homes tend to have the same size (6 feet 8 inches by 2 feet 6 inches) throughout the house, except for entrance doors, which most codes require to be 3 feet wide.

When replacing a door in an old house, where the openings may well be of nonstandard sizes, have a door made to fit the opening or buy a larger one and trim it to fit, removing an equal amount from each edge to preserve the door's symmetry.

Recessed molding

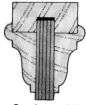

Overlay molding

Panel doors

Panel doors have a hardwood or softwood frame made with mortise-and-tenon or dowel joints. The frame is rabbeted or grooved to house the panels, which can be of solid wood, plywood, or glass. Doors constructed from hardboard, steel, or plastic panels are also available.

1 Muntins
These are the central vertical members of the door. They are jointed into the three cross rails.

2 Panels
These may be of solid wood or of plywood. They are held loosely in grooves in the frame to ensure that they can move without splitting. They stiffen the door.

3 Cross rails
The top, center, and bottom rails are tenoned into the stiles. In some doors, the mortise-and-tenon joints are replaced with dowel joints.

4 Stiles
These are the upright members at the sides of the door. They carry the hinges and the lock.

Panel-door moldings
The frame's inner edges may be plain or molded to form a decorative border. Small moldings are either machined on the frame before assembly or machined separately and nailed to the inside edge of the frame. An ordinary recessed molding (see far left) can shrink away from the frame and crack the paint. An overlay molding, which laps the frame, helps overcome this problem.

Flush doors

Most flush doors have a softwood frame faced with sheets of plywood or hardboard on both sides. Mainly used for interior doors, they're simple, light-weight, easy to hang, and inexpensive. Exterior flush doors have internal reinforcement blocks for lock hardware and mail slots.

1 Top and bottom rails
These are tenoned into the stiles.

2 Intermediate rails
These lighter rails, joined to the stiles, are notched to allow the passage of air, in order to prevent mold growth.

3 Lock blocks
A softwood block able to take a lockset is glued to each stile.

4 Panels
The plywood or hardboard panels are left plain for painting or finished with a wood veneer. Metal-skinned doors may be ordered specially.

Core material
Paper or cardboard honeycomb is often sandwiched between the panels in place of intermediate rails.

Panel door

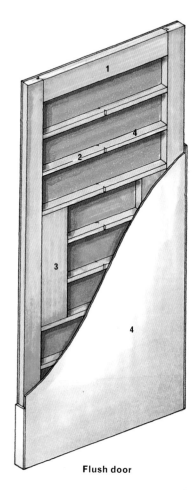

Flush door

Utility doors

These doors have a rustic look and are often found in old houses, outbuildings, attics, and basements. They are strong, easy to build, and when well maintained can last a very long time. These doors are usually hung with strap hinges.

1 Boards
Tongue-and-groove boards are nailed to cross-rail boards.

2 Strap hinges
Long strap hinges are used to carry the weight of a large exterior door.

3 Braces
These diagonal boards, sometimes notched into the cross rails, keep the door from sagging.

4 Cross rails
These are the support boards that the face boards are nailed to.

Framed utility door

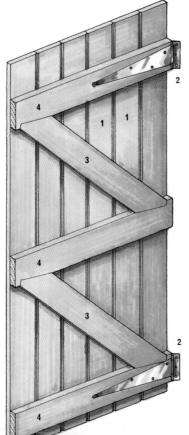

Basic utility door

Exterior doors

An exterior door is installed in a heavy wood frame consisting of a head jamb at the top, a sill at the bottom that's outfitted with a threshold, and side jambs, which are usually joined to the other pieces with dado joints.

In old houses, a section of the floor framing may need to be notched to accept the sill. But in newer homes, prehung exterior doors are made to rest on top of the subfloor. Thresholds come in different styles and are designed to seal the bottom of the door from the elements while allowing it to swing freely.

DOOR

WEATHERSTRIP

THRESHOLD

SILL

Exterior doorframe
1 Head jamb
2 Sill
3 Side jamb
4 Doorjamb rabbet
5 Notched floor framing

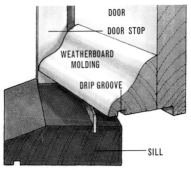

Installing a weatherboard

On some older houses, exterior doors don't have weather stripping installed and the sills are not outfitted with a watertight threshold (see pages 50–51). As a result, driving rain will be forced past the door and into the house. Of course, you can always replace an old door with a new one that comes with proper seals. But if you'd rather keep the door you have, you can create your own weather stripping.

A weatherboard is a molding that goes across the outside bottom edge of the door and sheds water that flows down the door away from the bottom of the door. To install one, measure the width of the opening between the doorstops and cut the molding to fit, shaving one end at a slight angle where it meets the doorframe on the lock side. This will allow it to clear the frame as the door swings open.

Use screws and a waterproof glue to attach the weatherboard to an unpainted door. When attaching one to a door that is already finished, apply a thick coat of primer to the back surface of the weatherboard to make a weatherproof seal. Then screw the weather stripping in place while the primer is still wet.

A door threshold should also have a weather bar installed as shown below. If the door is not typically exposed to driving rain, you can just install a weather bar and cut a rabbet in the bottom edge of the door that will seal against the bar.

DOOR

DOOR STOP

WEATHERBOARD MOLDING

DRIP GROOVE

SILL

Door with a weatherboard installed

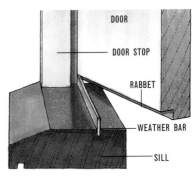

DOOR

DOOR STOP

RABBET

WEATHER BAR

SILL

Effects of weathering
A sadly neglected panel door that could have been preserved by applying a weatherboard before the deterioration had become widespread.

Maintaining brick and stone

At regular intervals and before you decorate the outside of your house, check the condition of the brick and stonework and carry out any necessary repairs. There's no reason why you can't paint brick or stonework, but you may want to restore painted masonry to its original condition. Although most paint strippers cannot cope with deeply textured surfaces, there are thick-paste paint removers that will peel away layers of old paint from masonry.

Paint-stained brickwork

Organic growth

Efflorescence

Treating new masonry

New brickwork or stonework should be left for about three months, until it is completely dry, before any further treatment is considered.

White powdery deposits called efflorescence may come to the surface over this period, but you can simply brush them off with a stiff-bristle brush or a piece of rough cloth. New masonry should be weatherproof and should not require further treatment, unless you want to apply paint.

Cleaning off unsightly mold

Colorful lichens growing on garden walls can be very attractive. Indeed, some people actively encourage their growth. However, since the spread of molds and lichens depends on damp conditions, it is not a good sign when they occur naturally on the walls of your house.

Try to identify the source of the problem before treating the growth. For example, if one side of the house never receives any sun, it will have little chance of drying out. Relieve the situation by cutting back overhanging trees or adjacent shrubs to increase ventilation to the wall.

Cracked or corroded gutters and downspouts leaking onto the wall are another common cause of organic growth. Feel behind the pipe with your fingers, or slip a hand mirror behind it to see if there's a leak.

Removing and neutralizing the growth

Scrape heavy organic growth from the bricks using a plastic putty knife. Then brush the masonry vigorously with a stiff-bristle brush. This can be an unpleasant, dusty job, so wear a face mask and safety glasses or goggles. Brush away from yourself so that debris doesn't land on your clothes.

Starting at the top of the wall, use a nylon brush to paint on a fungicidal solution, diluted according to the manufacturer's instructions. Apply the fungicide liberally and leave the wall to dry for 24 hours, then rinse the masonry thoroughly with clean water.

In extreme cases, give the wall two washes of fungicide, allowing 24 hours between applications and a further 24 hours before washing it down with clean water.

Removing efflorescence from masonry

Soluble salts within building materials such as cement, brick, and stone gradually migrate to the surface, along with the moisture, as a wall dries out. The result is a white crystalline deposit called efflorescence.

The same condition can occur on old masonry if it is subjected to more than average moisture. Efflorescence itself is not harmful, but the source of the damp must be identified and cured.

Brush the deposit from the wall regularly with a dry, stiff-bristle brush or coarse cloth until the crystals cease to form. Don't attempt to wash off the crystals—they will merely dissolve in the water and soak back into the wall. Above all, don't paint a wall that is still efflorescing, as this is a sign that it is still damp.

Masonry paints and clear sealants that let the wall breathe are not affected by the alkali content of the masonry, so they can be used without applying a primer. If you plan to use oil-based paint, coat the wall first with an alkali-resistant primer.

Cleaning masonry

Repointing masonry

You can spruce up old masonry by washing off surface grime. Strong solvents will harm certain types of stone, so consult an experienced local mason before applying anything other than water.

Washing the wall

Starting at the top of the wall, use a hose to spray water gently onto the masonry while you scrub it with a stiff-bristle brush **(1)**. Scrub heavy deposits with half a cup of ammonia added to a bucketful of water, then rinse again. Avoid soaking brick or stone when a frost is forecast.

Removing unsightly stains

Soften tar, grease, and oil stains using a household kitchen cleanser. Check the manufacturer's instructions for proper application and rinsing.

To remove a patch of spilled paint, use paint stripper. Follow the manufacturer's recommendations and wear old clothes, gloves, and goggles.

Stipple the stripper onto the rough texture **(2)**. Leave it for about 10 minutes, then remove the softened paint with a scraper. Gently scrub the residue out of deeper crevices with a stiff-bristle brush and water. Then rinse the wall with clean water.

If any paint remains in the crevices, dip your brush in stripper and gently scrub it into the problem areas. Use small circular strokes. After the stripper has set, wash it off and repeat if necessary.

1 Remove dirt and dust by washing

2 Stipple paint stripper onto paint

Frost action and erosion tend to break down the mortar pointing of brickwork and stonework. The mortar eventually falls out, exposing the open joints to wind and rain, which drive dampness through the wall to the inside of the house. Replacing defective mortar is a straightforward but time-consuming task. Tackle a small area at a time, using a ready-mixed mortar made for this job.

Applying the mortar

Scrape out the old pointing with a thin wooden stick to a depth of about ½ inch. Use a cold chisel and a hammer to dislodge sections that are firmly embedded; then brush out the joints with a stiff-bristle brush.

Spray the wall with water to make sure the bricks or stones will not absorb too much moisture from the fresh mortar. Mix up some mortar in a bucket and transfer it to a hawk. If you are mixing your own mortar, use these proportions: 1 part cement, 1 part lime, 6 parts builder's sand.

Pick up a small sausage of mortar on the back of a pointing trowel and push it firmly into the upright joints. This can be difficult to do without the mortar dropping off, so hold the hawk under each joint to catch it.

Try not to smear the face of the bricks with mortar, as it will stain. Use the same method for the horizontal joints. The actual shape of the pointing is not vital at this stage.

Once the mortar is firm enough to retain a thumbprint, it is ready for shaping. Because it is important that you shape the joints at exactly the right moment, you may have to point the work in stages in order to complete the wall. Shape the joints to match existing brickwork, or choose a profile suitable for the prevailing weather conditions in your area.

Once you have shaped the joints, wait until the pointing has almost hardened, then brush the wall to remove traces of surplus mortar from the surface of the masonry.

Shaping the mortar joints

Flush joint This is the easiest profile to produce. Scrape the mortar flush, using the edge of your trowel, then stipple the joints with a stiff-bristle brush.

Rubbed (concave) joint This joint is ideal for an old wall with bricks that are not of sufficiently good quality to take a crisp joint. Bricklayers make a rubbed joint using a jointer, a tool shaped like a sled runner with a handle. Its semicircular blade is run along the joints. Improvise a tool by bending a length of metal tube or rod (use the curved section only, or you will gouge the mortar). Scrape the mortar flush first, then drag the tool along the joints. Finish the vertical joints, then shape the horizontal ones. Having shaped the joints, stipple them with a brush so that they look like weathered joints.

Raked joint A raked joint is used to emphasize the bonding pattern of a brick wall. It is not suitable for an exposed site where the wall takes a lot of weathering.

Rake out the new joints to a depth of about ¼ inch, and then compress the mortar by smoothing it lightly with a piece of lath or wood dowel.

Weatherstruck joint The sloping profile is intended to shed rainwater from the wall. Shape the mortar with the edge of a pointing trowel. Start with the vertical joints, sloping them either to the right or to the left (but be consistent). Then shape the horizontal joints, allowing the mortar to spill out at the base of each joint.

Finish the joint by cutting off the excess mortar with a Frenchman, a tool that has a narrow blade with the tip bent at 90 degrees. Use a board to guide the Frenchman along the joints and nail scraps of wood at each end to hold the board off the wall. Align the board with the bottom of the horizontal joints, then draw the tool along it to trim off the excess mortar.

• Mortar joints
The joints shown here are commonly used for brickwork. Flush or rubbed joints are best for most stonework, though sometimes raised mortar joints are used with stone.

Flush

Rubbed

Raked

Weatherstruck

Repairing masonry

Spalled masonry

Cracked masonry may simply be the result of cement-rich mortar being unable to absorb slight movements within the building. However, it could also be a sign of a more serious problem—sinking foundations, for example. Don't just ignore the symptoms; investigate immediately and undertake the necessary repairs as soon as possible.

Filling cracked masonry

If a brick or stone wall has substantial cracks, consult a local builder or home inspector to ascertain the cause. If a crack proves to be stable, you can carry out some repairs yourself.

Cracked mortar can be removed and repointed in the normal way, but a crack that splits the bricks cannot be repaired neatly, and the damaged masonry should be replaced by a mason.

Cracks across a painted wall can be filled with mortar that has been mixed with a little bonding agent to help it stick. Before you make the repair, wet the damaged masonry with a hose to encourage the mortar to flow deeply into the crack.

Cracks may follow mortar only

Cracked bricks could signify serious faults

Priming brickwork for painting

Brickwork will need to be primed only if it is showing signs of efflorescence or spalling. An alkali-resistant primer will guard against efflorescence. A stabilizing solution will bind crumbling masonry and also help to seal it.

When you are painting a wall for the first time with masonry paint, you may find that the first coat is difficult to apply due to the suction of the dry, porous brick. Thin the first coat slightly with water or solvent.

Waterproofing masonry

Colorless water-repellent fluids are intended to make masonry impervious to water without coloring it or stopping it from breathing, which is important because it allows moisture within the walls to dry out.

Prepare the surface before applying the fluid: Repair any cracks in bricks or pointing and remove organic growth; then allow the wall to dry out thoroughly. Cover nearby plants.

The fumes from water-repellents can be dangerous if inhaled, so be sure to wear a proper respirator as recommended by the manufacturer. Also, wear eye protection.

Apply the fluid generously with a large paintbrush, from the bottom up,

Replacing a spalled brick
Having mortared the top and one end, slip the new brick into the hole you have cut.

and stipple it into the joints. Apply a second coat as soon as the first has been absorbed to ensure that there are no bare patches where water could seep in. To be sure that you are covering the wall properly, use a sealant containing a fugitive dye, which disappears after a specified period of time.

Carefully paint up to surrounding woodwork. If you accidentally splash sealant onto it, wash it immediately with a cloth dampened with solvent.

If you need to treat a whole house, it may be worth hiring a company that can spray the sealant. Make sure the workers rig up screens to prevent overspray from drifting across to your neighbors' property.

Moisture that has penetrated soft masonry will expand in icy weather, flaking off the outer face of brickwork and stonework. The result, known as spalling, not only looks unattractive but also allows water to seep into the wall.

If spalling is localized, cut out and replace the bricks or stones. The sequence below describes how to repair spalled brickwork, but the process is similar for a stone wall.

Where spalling is extensive, the only practical solution is to accept its less-than-perfect appearance, repoint the masonry, and apply a clear water-repellent that will protect the wall from further damage while allowing it to breathe.

Spalled bricks caused by frost damage

Replacing a spalled brick

Use a cold chisel and hammer to remove the pointing surrounding the brick, then chop out the brick itself. If the brick is difficult to remove, drill numerous holes in it with a large-diameter masonry bit; then chop out the brick with a cold chisel and hammer. It should crumble, enabling you to remove the pieces easily.

To fit the replacement brick, first dampen the opening and spread mortar on the base and one side. Then dampen the replacement brick, cover the top and one end with mortar and slot the brick into the hole (see far left). Shape the pointing to match the surrounding brickwork.

If you can't find a replacement brick in the right color, remove the spalled brick carefully, turn it around to the undamaged side, and reinsert it.

Repairing stucco

Brickwork is sometimes clad with a smooth or roughcast cement-based stucco, both for improved weatherproofing and to provide a decorative finish. Stucco is susceptible to the effects of damp and frost, which can cause cracking, bulging, and staining. Before you paint a stuccoed wall, make any necessary repairs and clean off surface dirt, mold growth, and flaky material for a finish that will last.

Cracked stucco allows moisture to penetrate

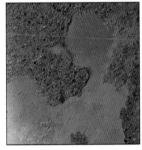

Pebbledash can separate and fall off walls

Leaky gutters can cause rust stains

Repairing defects

Before you repair cracked stucco, have a home inspector or engineer check the wall for any structural faults that may have contributed to the problem. Apply a stabilizing solution if the wall is dusty.

You can ignore fine hairline cracks if you intend to paint the wall with a reinforced masonry paint, but scrape out larger cracks with a cold chisel. Dampen them with water and fill flush with a cement-based exterior filler. Fill any major cracks with a stucco made of 1 part cement, 2 parts lime, and 9 parts builder's sand, plus a little bonding agent to help it stick to the wall.

Bulges in stucco normally indicate that the stucco has separated from the masonry

Reinforcing a crack

To prevent a crack in stucco from opening up again, you can reinforce the repair with a polyester membrane embedded in a primer designed for making stucco patches. When you're done patching, you will need to cover the wall with a textured paint in order to disguise the repair.

To patch cracks, begin by scraping out the crack to remove loose material, then wet it. Fill just over the surface with a mortar mix of 1 part cement and 4 parts builder's sand. When this has stiffened, scrape it

Patching pebbledash

For additional weatherproofing, sometimes small stones are stuck to a thin coat of stucco over a thicker base coat. This process is known as pebbledashing. If water gets behind pebbledashing, one or both layers may separate. Chip off any loose stucco to a sound base, then seal it with stabilizer. If necessary, repair the scratch coat (bottom coat) of stucco.

You can simulate the texture of pebble-dash with a thick paste made from bonding agent. Mix 1 part cement-paint powder with 3 parts plasterer's sand. Stir in 1 part of bonding agent diluted with 3 parts water to form a thick, creamy paste. Load a brush and scrub the paste onto the bare surface.

Apply a second generous coat of paste,

or sheathing underneath. Tap the wall gently to find the extent of these hollow areas, then remove the material until you reach sound edges. Use a chisel to undercut the perimeter of each hole except for the bottom edge, which should be left square so that it does not collect water.

Brush out the debris, then apply a coat of bonding agent. When it becomes tacky, trowel on a layer of 1 : 1 : 6 stucco, about ½ inch thick. Leave the stucco to set firm, then scratch it to form a key. The next day, fill the hole flush with a weaker mix (1 : 1 : 9) and smooth the surface with a wooden float, using circular strokes.

flush. When the mortar has hardened, brush on a generous coat of the primer, making sure it extends at least 4 inches on both sides of the crack. Embed strips of polyester membrane (sold for use with the primer) into the coating, using a stippling and brushing action **(1)**. While it is still wet, feather the edges of the primer with a foam roller **(2)**, bedding the membrane into it. After 24 hours, apply a second coat of primer and feather with the roller. When the primer is dry, apply textured coating.

stippling it to form a coarse texture. Leave it for about 15 minutes to firm up. Then, with a loaded brush, stipple it to match the texture of the pebbles. Let the paste harden fully before painting the repair.

If you want to leave the pebble-dash unpainted, make a patch using replacement pebbles. The result may not be a perfect match, but could save you from having to paint the entire wall. Cut back the damaged area and apply a stucco scratch coat followed by a finish coat. While this is still wet, fling pebbles onto the surface from a dustpan. You may have to repeat the process until the coverage is even.

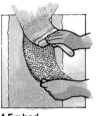

1 Embed membrane

2 Feather with roller

Stipple texture

• Removing rust stains
Faulty downspouts or gutters can result in rusty streaks on a stuccoed wall. Before painting, prime the areas with a stain-blocking sealer. Rust marks on a pebbledashed wall are sometimes caused by iron pyrites in the aggregate. Chip out the pyrites with a cold chisel, then seal the stain.

Painted masonry

Stripping painted masonry

Painted masonry inside the house is usually in fairly good condition, and apart from a good cleaning to remove dust and grease and a light sanding to give a key for the new finish, there is little else you need to do. Outside, however, it's a different matter. Exterior surfaces, subjected to extremes of heat, cold, and rain, are likely to be affected to some degree by stains, flaking, and chalkiness.

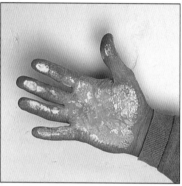
A chalky surface needs stabilizing

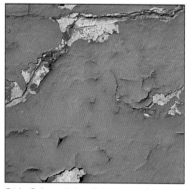
Strip flaky paintwork to a sound surface

Chimney stained by tar deposits from the flue

Curing a chalky surface

Rub the palm of your hand lightly over the surface of the wall to see if it is chalky. If the paint rubs off as a powdery deposit, treat the wall before you repaint.

Brush the surface with a stiff-bristle brush, then paint the whole wall liberally with a stabilizing primer, which will bind the chalky surface so that paint will adhere to it. Use a white stabilizing primer, which can also serve as an undercoat. Clean any splashes from surrounding woodwork with solvent.

If the wall is very dusty, apply a second coat of stabilizer after about 16 hours. Wait another 16 hours before applying paint.

Dealing with flaky paint

Poor surface preparation or incompatible paint and preparatory treatments are common causes of flaky paintwork. Damp walls will also cause flaking, so cure the damp and let the wall dry out before further treatment.

A new coat of paint will not bind to a flaky surface, so attend to this before you start painting. Use a paint scraper and a stiff-bristle brush to remove all loose material. Coarse sandpaper should finish the job, or at least feather the edges of any stubborn patches. Stabilize the surface as for chalky walls before repainting.

Treat tar stains with a blocking sealer.

Treating a stained chimney

If the outlines of brick courses show up as brown staining on a painted chimney, you can be sure it is caused by a breakdown of the internal flue liner of the chimney. Defective lining allows tar deposits to migrate through the mortar joints to the outer paintwork. To solve the problem, first repair the old flue liner or install a new one; then treat the brown stains with a stain-blocking primer/sealer before applying a fresh coat of paint.

In the past, even sound brickwork was often painted, simply to brighten up a house. In some areas of the country where painted masonry is traditional, there is every reason to continue with the practice. Indeed, houses with soft, inferior brickwork were frequently painted when they were built in order to protect them from the weather—and to strip them now could have serious consequences. But if the brick on your house is in good condition and doesn't need paint to protect it, then removing the paint is an option—albeit an expensive one.

Restoring painted brickwork to its natural condition is not an easy task. It is generally a messy business involving the use of toxic materials that have to be handled with care and disposed of safely. Extensive scaffolding may be required, and most important, getting the masonry entirely clean demands considerable experience. For all these reasons, it is advisable to hire professionals to do the work for you.

To determine whether the outcome is likely to be successful, ask the company you are thinking of hiring to strip an inconspicuous patch of masonry, using the chemicals they recommend for the job. The results may indicate that it is better to repaint—in which case, choose a good-quality masonry paint that will let moisture within the walls evaporate.

A painted wall in need of restoration.

In common with other building materials, concrete suffers from the effects of damp—spalling and efflorescence—and related defects, such as cracking and crumbling. Repairs can usually be made in much the same way as for brickwork and stucco, although there are some special considerations you should be aware of. If the damage is widespread, resurface the concrete before painting.

Sealing concrete

New concrete has a high alkali content. Efflorescence can therefore develop on the surface as it dries out. When treating efflorescence on concrete, follow the procedure recommended for brickwork. A porous concrete wall should be waterproofed with a clear sealant on the exterior. Some reinforced masonry paints will cover tar satisfactorily, but it will bleed through most paints unless you prime first with a bonding agent diluted 50 percent with water. Alternatively, use a stain-blocking primer/sealer.

Cleaning dirty concrete

You can scrub dirty concrete with water (as described for brickwork), but when a concrete driveway or garage floor is stained with patches of oil or grease, you will need to apply an oil-and-grease remover. This is a detergent that is normally diluted with an equal amount of water, but can be used full strength on heavy staining. Brush on the solution liberally, then scrub the surface with a stiff-bristle brush. Rinse off with clean water. It is advisable to wear eye protection. Keep all windows and doors open when working indoors.

It is worth soaking up fresh oil spillages immediately with dry sand or sawdust to prevent permanent stains.

Binding dusty concrete

Concrete is troweled when it is laid to give it a flat finish. If the troweling is overdone, cement is brought to the surface; and when the concrete dries out, this thin layer begins to break up, producing a loose, dusty surface. Though not always necessary, it is generally recommended that you paint on a concrete-floor sealer before applying any paint. Treat a dusty concrete wall with stabilizing primer.

Repairing cracks and holes

Rake out and brush away loose debris from cracks and holes in concrete. If the crack is less than ¼ inch wide, open it up a little with a cold chisel so it will accept a filling (see far right). Undercut the edges to form a lip so that the filler will grip. To fill a hole in concrete, add a fine aggregate such as gravel to a sand-and-cement mix. Make sure the fresh concrete sticks in shallow depressions by priming the damaged surface with 3 parts bonding agent and 1 part water. When the primed surface is tacky, trowel in the concrete and smooth it. See also cement-based fillers (far right).

Treating spalled concrete

When concrete breaks up, or spalls, due to the action of frost, the process is accelerated as steel reinforcement is exposed and begins to corrode. Fill the concrete as described above, but paint the metalwork first with a rust-inhibiting primer.

Spalling concrete

An uneven or pitted concrete floor must be made level before you apply any form of floorcovering. You can do this fairly easily yourself using a self-leveling compound, but make sure the surface is dry before proceeding.

Testing for damp

If you suspect a concrete floor is damp, make a simple test by laying a small piece of polyethelene on the concrete and sealing it all around with tape. After one or two days, inspect it for any traces of moisture on the underside.

If the test indicates that treatment is required, apply three coats of heavy-duty, moisture-cured polyurethane sealant. No longer than 4 hours should elapse between coats. The floor should be as dry as possible so that it is porous enough for the first coat to penetrate. If necessary, use a fan heater to help dry the floor.

Before applying a self-leveling compound, lightly scatter dry sand over the last coat of sealant while it is still wet. Allow it to harden for three days, then brush off loose residual sand.

Applying a self-leveling compound

Self-leveling compound is supplied as a powder that you mix with water. Be sure the floor is clean and free from dampness (see previous section), then pour some of the compound in the corner that is farthest away from the door. Spread the compound with a trowel until it is about ⅛ inch thick, then leave it to seek its own level. Continue across the floor, joining the areas of compound until the entire surface is covered. You can walk on the floor after an hour or so without damaging it, but leave the compound to harden for a few days before laying a permanent floorcovering.

● **Leave a new floor to dry out.** A new floor with a vapor barrier installed should be left to dry out for 6 months before any impermeable covering, such as sheet vinyl or tiles, is laid.

● **Cement-based exterior fillers.** As an alternative to making up your own sand-and-cement mix, you can buy a cement-based exterior filler for patching holes in concrete and rebuilding broken corners. When mixed with water, the filler remains workable for 10 to 20 minutes. Just before it sets hard, smooth or scrape the filler level.

Filling cracks. Before you fill a narrow crack, open it up and undercut the edges using a cold chisel.

Applying self-leveling compound. Pour the compound and spread it with a trowel.

Painting exterior masonry

Take sensible precautions when using oil-based paints:

- Ensure good ventilation indoors while applying a finish and while it is drying. Wear a respirator if you suffer from breathing disorders.
- Don't smoke while painting or in the vicinity of drying paint.
- Contain paint spillages outside with sand or soil, and don't allow any paint to enter a sewer drain.
- If you splash paint in your eyes, flush them with copious amounts of water, with your lids held open. See a doctor immediately.
- Always wear gloves if you have sensitive skin. Use a skin cleanser to remove paint from your skin, or wash it off with warm soapy water. Don't use paint thinners to clean your skin.
- Keep all finishes and thinners out of reach of children. If a child swallows a substance, don't make any attempt to induce vomiting—seek medical treatment instead.

Preparing paint

Whether you are using paint you've just bought, or some left over from a previous job, there are a few basic rules to observe before you apply it.

- Wipe dust from the paint can, then pry off the lid with a can-opening tool or a flat-blade screwdriver.
- Gently stir the paint with a wooden stick to blend the pigment and the medium.
- If a skin has formed on paint, cut around the edge with a knife and lift the skin out in one piece with a stick. It's a good idea to store the can upside down so a skin cannot form on top of the paint.
- If the paint is old, it should be strained before use. Just put a scrap piece of muslin over the lip of a paint bucket and tie it under the lip. Pour the old paint into the filter.

- **Disposing of unwanted paint.** Before you wash your brushes and rollers, wipe them on newspaper to remove as much paint as possible. Ask your local authority about facilities for disposing of waste paint and cans.

Strain old paint. If you are using leftover paint, filter it through a piece of muslin or old tights tied over the rim of a paint bucket.

Resealing the lid. Wipe the rim of the can clean before you replace the lid. Tap a metal lid down all around with a hammer over a wood block.

The outside walls of houses are painted for two main reasons: to give a bright, clean appearance, and to protect the surface from the weather. What you use as a finish and how you apply it depend on what the walls are made from, their condition, and the degree of protection they need. Bricks are traditionally left bare but may require a coat of paint if they've been painted before. Stuccoed walls are often painted to brighten the naturally dull, gray color of the cement; pebble-dashed surfaces may need a colorful coat to disguise unsightly patches. Or you may, of course, simply want to change the present color of your walls for a fresh appearance.

Working with a plan

Before you start painting outside masonry walls, plan your time carefully. Depending on the amount of preparation that is required, even a small house will take a few weeks to complete.

It is preferable, though, to tackle the whole job at once, since the weather may upset your timetable.

You can split the work into separate stages with days (or even weeks) in between, provided you divide the walls into manageable sections. Use window frames and doorframes, bays, and corners of walls to form break lines that will disguise joints.

Start at the top of the house, working from right to left, if you are right-handed.

- **Black dot denotes compatibility.** All surfaces must be clean, sound, dry, and free from organic growth.

FINISHES FOR MASONRY

	Cement paint	Exterior latex paint	Reinforced latex paint	Solvent-thinned masonry paint	Textured coating	Floor paint
SUITABLE TO COVER						
Brick	●	●	●	●	●	●
Stone	●	●	●	●	●	●
Concrete	●	●	●	●	●	●
Stucco	●	●	●	●	●	●
Exposed-aggregate concrete	●	●	●	●	●	●
Asbestos cement	●					
Latex paint		●	●	●	●	●
Oil-based paint		●	●	●	●	●
Cement paint	●	●	●	●	●	●
DRYING TIME: HOURS						
Touch-dry	1–2	1–2	2–3	1–2	6	2–3
Recoatable	24	4	24	24	24–48	12–24
THINNERS: SOLVENTS						
Water-thinned	●	●	●		●	
Solvent-thinned				●		●
NUMBER OF COATS						
Normal conditions	2	2	1–2	2	1	1–2
COVERAGE: DEPENDING ON WALL TEXTURE						
Sq. ft. per quart		150–400	120–250	120–225		180–550
Sq. ft. per pound	30–75				20–40	
METHOD OF APPLICATION						
Brush	●	●	●	●	●	●
Roller	●	●	●	●	●	●
Spray gun	●	●	●	●	●	●

Paints suitable for exterior masonry

There are various grades of paint suitable for painting and protecting exterior masonry that take into account economy, finish, durability, and coverage. Use the chart on the facing page for quick reference.

Cement paint

Cement paint is supplied as a dry powder to which water is added. It is based on white cement, but pigments are added to produce a range of colors. Cement paint is one of the cheaper paints suitable for exterior use. Spray new or porous surfaces with water, then apply two coats.

Mixing cement paint Shake or roll the container to loosen the powder, then add two parts of powder to one part of water in a clean bucket. Stir it to a smooth paste, then add a little more water until you get a full-bodied, creamy consistency. Don't mix more than you can use in an hour, or it will start to dry.

Adding an aggregate When you're painting a wall that has been treated with a stabilizing solution so its porosity is substantially reduced, it's a good idea to add clean sand to the mix to give it body. This also provides added protection for an exposed wall and helps to cover dark colors. If the sand changes the color of the paint, add it to the first coat only. Use one part sand to four parts of powder, stirring it in when the paint is still in a pastelike consistency.

Masonry paints

Water-based masonry paint Most masonry paints are water based, with additives that prevent mold growth. Although they are supplied ready for use, on porous walls it pays to thin the first coat with 20 percent water. Follow up with one or two full-strength coats, depending on the color of the paint.

Water-based masonry paints must be applied during fairly good weather.

Solvent-based masonry paints Some masonry paints are thinned with mineral spirits or with a special solvent. But unlike most oil paints they are moisture-vapor permeable, so that the wall is able to breathe. It is often best to thin the first coat with 15 percent mineral spirits, but check the manufacturer's recommendations.

Solvent-based paints can be applied in practically any weather conditions, provided it is not actually raining.

Reinforced masonry paint Masonry paint that has powdered mica or a similar fine aggregate added to it dries with a textured finish that is extremely weatherproof. Although large cracks and holes must be filled prior to painting, reinforced masonry paint will cover hairline cracks and crazing.

Textured coating

A thick textured coating applied to exterior walls forms a thoroughly weatherproof coating that can be painted over to match other colors. The usual preparation is necessary, and brickwork needs to be pointed flush.

Large cracks should be filled, although a textured coating will cover fine cracks. The paste is either brushed or rolled onto the wall, then left to harden, forming an even texture.

Concrete floor paint

Floor paints are formulated to withstand hard wear. They are especially suitable for concrete garage or workshop floors, but they are also used for stone steps and other concrete structures. They can also be used inside for playroom floors.

The floor must be clean, dry, and free from oil or grease. If the concrete is freshly laid, allow it to mature for at least two months before painting. In most cases, it is advisable to prime powdery or porous floors with a concrete sealer, but check the manufacturer's recommendations first.

The best way to paint a large area is to use a paintbrush around the edges, then fit an extension handle to a paint roller for the bulk of the floor.

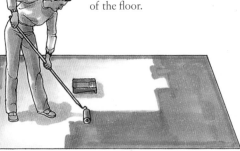

Apply paint with a roller on an extension handle

Paint in manageable sections.
You can't hope to paint an entire house in one session, so divide each side into manageable sections to disguise the joints. The horizontal molding divides the front of this house neatly into two sections, and the raised door and window trim form convenient break lines.

Techniques for painting masonry

1 Cut in with a gentle scrubbing motion

2 Protect downspouts with newspaper

3 Use a banister brush.
Tackle deeply textured wall surfaces with a banister brush.

Using the correct roller
When painting heavy textures, use a roller that has a deep pile. Switch to a medium pile for light textures and smooth surfaces.

1 Spray onto the apex of outside corners

Spray gun
Rent a high-quality spray gun and a small portable compressor.

2 Spray inside corners as separate surfaces

Using paintbrushes

Choose a brush that is 4 to 6 inches wide for painting walls; larger ones are heavy and tiring to use. A good-quality brush with coarse bristles will last longer on rough walls. For effective coverage, apply the paint with vertical strokes, crisscrossed with horizontal ones. You will find it necessary to stipple paint into textured surfaces.

Cutting in Painting up to features such as a door, window, and baseboard trim is known as cutting in. On a smooth surface, you should be able to paint a reasonably straight edge following the line of the trim—but it's difficult to apply the paint to a heavily textured wall with a normal brush stroke. Don't just apply more paint in the hope of overcoming the problem; instead, touch only the tip of the brush to the wall, using a gentle scrubbing action

Using a paint roller

A roller will apply paint three times as fast as a brush. Use a deep-pile roller for heavy textures, and one with a medium pile for lightly textured or smooth walls. Rollers wear out very quickly on rough walls, so have a spare sleeve handy. When painting with a roller, vary the angle of

Using a spray gun

Spraying is the quickest and most efficient way to apply paint to a large expanse of wall. But you will have to mask all the areas you don't want to paint, using newspaper and masking tape, and set drop cloths to prevent overspray.

Thin the paint by about 10 percent, and set the spray gun according to the manufacturer's instructions to suit the particular paint. Make sure to wear a respirator.

Hold the gun about 9 inches away from the wall and keep it moving with even,

(1), then brush out from the edge to spread excess paint once the texture is filled. Wipe splashed paint from any trim with a cloth dampened with the appropriate thinner.

Painting behind downspouts To protect downspouts, tape a piece of newspaper around them. Stipple behind the downspout with a brush **(2)**, then move the newspaper down the pipe to mask the next section.

Painting with a banister brush Use a banister brush **(3)** to paint deep textures such as pebble dash. Pour some paint into a roller tray and dip the brush in to load the bristles. Scrub the paint onto the wall, using circular strokes to work it into the uneven surface.

the stroke to ensure even coverage. Use a brush to cut into angles and obstructions.

A paint tray is difficult to use at the top of an extension ladder, unless you install a support bracket.

parallel passes. Slightly overlap each pass and try to keep the gun pointing directly at the surface. Trigger the gun just before each pass, and release it at the end of the stroke.

To cover a large blank wall evenly, spray it with vertical bands of paint, overlapping each band by about 4 inches.

Spray outside corners by aiming the gun directly at the apex so that paint falls evenly on both surfaces **(1)**. When two walls meet at an inside corner, spray each surface separately **(2)**.

Roofs

Traditionally most roofs were made with rafters that were cut and installed on site, and this is still the way many roofs are built, especially when usable attic space is required. But most roofs today are built with trusses. These units are fabricated in factories and simply nailed in place on site. Trusses are strong, stable, and usually more economical than rafter roofs. But installing them generally eliminates the attic space.

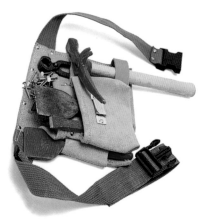

Basic construction

The framework of an ordinary roof is based on a triangle, the most rigid and economical form for a loadbearing structure. The weight of the roofing and sheathing is carried either by prefabricated trusses, or by framing members called rafters, which are installed in opposing pairs. Rafters are joined at the top to a central ridge board running the length of the roof. The bottom ends of the rafters are attached to the top plates of the walls.

To stop the roof's weight from pushing the walls out, horizontal members tie the walls together and the rafters together. The bottom ones, installed next to the rafters on the top plates, are the ceiling joists. Members that are nailed to the sides of the rafters, closer to the ridge, are called collar ties.

Roof types

There are many different roof styles, often used in combination. Most of them, however, fall into these basic classifications:

Flat Roof Flat roofs may be supported on joists to which the ceiling material is also attached, or they may be constructed using trusses which have parallel top and bottom members supported by triangular bracing in between. Most flat roofs actually have a slight slope, formed by the roofing material, to provide drainage.

Shed Roof This is the simplest type of roof. Sometimes it is called a lean-to roof. Inside the structure, the ceiling may be attached directly to the rafters to form a sloping surface, or be supported by horizontal joists to form a flat surface.

Gable Roof Two shed roofs joined together form the classic gable roof, the most commonly used roof in residential construction today. Gable roofs are simple and economical to build and have excellent loadbearing and drainage capabilities. The end walls under the roof are nonloadbearing.

Gambrel Roof By breaking the slope of a gable roof into two differently pitched sections, more headroom becomes available in the attic area beneath the rafters. The gambrel design also makes the construction of a wide roof easier because shorter lengths of lumber can be used in combination to span large widths.

Hip Roofs By sloping the ends of a gable roof toward the center, a hip roof is formed. This roof style provides a protective overhang on all four sides of the building.

Intersecting Roofs Many houses combine the same or different roof types, built at angles to one another, to form L- or U-shaped floor plans, and other shapes.

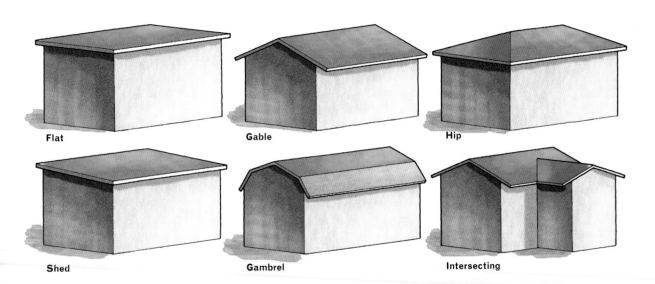

Flat   Gable   Hip

Shed   Gambrel   Intersecting

Roof construction

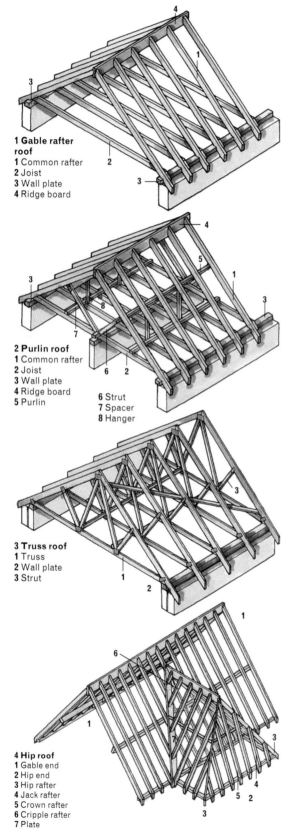

1 Gable rafter roof
1 Common rafter
2 Joist
3 Wall plate
4 Ridge board

2 Purlin roof
1 Common rafter
2 Joist
3 Wall plate
4 Ridge board
5 Purlin
6 Strut
7 Spacer
8 Hanger

3 Truss roof
1 Truss
2 Wall plate
3 Strut

4 Hip roof
1 Gable end
2 Hip end
3 Hip rafter
4 Jack rafter
5 Crown rafter
6 Cripple rafter
7 Plate

A s mentioned earlier, most roof design is based on the triangle. If all the legs of a triangle are firmly attached to adjacent legs, it is very difficult to distort the shape. But holding its shape is not all that a roof system has to do. It must also keep the side walls of the house from spreading apart. To do both, the side walls and the rafters must be joined together with ceiling joists and collar ties to produce a sound structure.

Gable rafter roof

A gable roof **(1)** is the basic design for residential roofs. It can be made with trusses (see left) or traditional rafters. Even though building a gable roof is a lot of work, its design is the essence of simplicity: Two flat planes are joined together to form a peaked structure.

The top of the framework is called the ridge and it is formed by the junction of the rafters from both sides and a ridge board that runs perpendicular to the rafters. The ridge is supported by the rafters and the rafters are supported by the outside walls. If the joint between the rafters and the top wall plate is weak the roof will fail.

To tie the rafters together and form the basic triangle, and to keep the walls from spreading, ceiling joists are nailed to the top plates and the sides of the rafters. These joints are also crucial to the overall strength of the roof.

Purlin roof

In a purlin roof **(2)**, horizontal beams called purlins link the rafters, running midway between the outside wall and the ridge.

The ends of the purlins are supported at the gable wall or, in the case of a hip roof, by hip rafters (see left). The purlins effectively reduce the unsupported span of the rafters, which allows relatively lightweight lumber to be used for the rafters. In order to keep the size of the purlins to a minimum, diagonal struts are installed in opposing pairs to brace them, usually every fourth or fifth rafter. The struts transfer some of the roof weight back to a center loadbearing wall. This type of roof is rarely built anymore; but looking at it suggests the beginning of truss roof construction.

Truss roof

A truss roof **(3)** allows for a relatively wide span and dispenses with the need for a loadbearing partition wall. Like rafters, trusses transfer the entire weight of the roof to the exterior walls.

In most new housing, trusses are computer designed for economy and strength. Each truss combines two roof chords (corresponding to rafters), a bottom chord (to function like a ceiling joist), and struts that join and brace the chords. All the joints are butt joints reinforced with heavy-duty plate connectors. Trusses are usually spaced on 24-inch centers so standard roof sheathing panels will fit the layout without being cut.

Truss roofs are relatively lightweight and can span greater distances than rafter roofs, because trusses don't require a partition wall to support the ceiling joists.

Hip roofs

Hip roofs **(4)** are often used for additions to gable roofs to break up the simplicity of a straight roof. Additional framing members include hip rafters, jack rafters, crown rafters, and cripple rafters. The illustration (left) shows a gable roof and a smaller hip roof added to the side. The points where the two meet are called valleys. The valleys collect and direct rainwater from both roof surfaces to the gutters.

Roof elements

The style of a roof is classified not only by the basic shape of the structure but also by the detailing along the eaves. The eaves are where the ends of the rafter meet the exterior walls. The basic eaves vari-ations are shown below.

Flush eaves When the ends of the rafters are cut flush with the outside wall of the house and covered with a fascia board, the eaves are called flush **(1)**. Gutters are installed directly on the fascia.

Open eaves If the ends of the rafters extend beyond the outside of the wall, and aren't covered with a fascia board, the eaves are referred to as open **(2)**. This style of eaves is no longer very popular in new construction. But many older houses have them, and frequently the ends have designs cut or carved in them. Gutters are usually in brackets nailed to the top of the rafters before the roofing is installed.

Closed eaves A closed eave **(3)** is a combination of the flush and the open approaches. The rafters extend past the outside wall, like open eaves. But they are enclosed with a fascia board, like a flush eave. A soffit board is installed under the rafters to close the space.

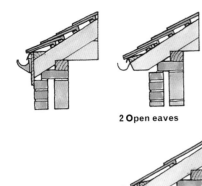

2 Open eaves

3 Closed eaves

Checking your roof

A roof structure can fail if its members are exposed to high moisture levels and insect attacks. Failure can also result from overloading due to the use of undersized framing lumber, roofing that's too heavy for the structure, or modifications to the framework to add stairs, dormers, or an attic room without proper reinforcement. A sagging roof, which indicates serious damage, can usually be seen from the ground.

Inspecting your roof

The roof should be inspected from inside. Do this annually to check for any leaks and the presence of destructive insects. For the inspection to be useful, you must have a good source of light. If your attic has no lighting, use an extension cord with a lamp or work light on the end. If the attic has no floor, walk only on the top edges of the joists.

Moisture problems

Rot in roof members is a serious problem which should be corrected by professionals. Rot is caused by damp conditions that encourage the growth of fungi that can destroy the wood.

Inspect the roof sheathing closely for loose or damaged boards or panels in the general area of the rot. Keep in mind that water may be penetrating the roof at a higher level and running down to the rotted area. The source of water damage is not always obvious.

If the rot is close to the intersection of two roofs, you should suspect the flashing. Rot can also be caused by too much condensation in the roof space, a problem that's usually fixed by installing more ventilation.

You should also inspect all the openings in the roof to make sure water isn't leaking around them. This includes the main plumbing vent stack, roof vents, and chimneys. If they're accessible, check the eaves to see if there's evidence that water has backed up due to ice dams or clogged downspouts. Many older homes have windows in the attic that should be checked for leaks and faulty glazing.

Strengthening the roof

A roof that shows signs of sagging may have to be jacked and braced. But some sagging roofs have already been stabilized, so they don't present a structural problem. They may look bad but aren't in any danger of collapsing. In some old buildings a slightly sagging roof line is even considered attractive.

Consult an engineer if you suspect a roof is weak. Apart from a sagging roofline, the walls under the eaves should be inspected for bulging out of plumb. Bulging can occur where improperly framed window openings are close to the eaves, weakening that section of the wall. Walls can also bulge because the roof weight is spreading them apart. This is usually the result of poor joints between rafters and ceiling joists.

A lightly constructed roof can be made stronger by adding extra structural members. This work can often be done from inside the attic. But when the damage is severe, the roofing and sheathing have to be stripped from the outside before the repairs can be made.

This is work for professionals. Make sure they have liability insurance before hiring them.

A well-constructed roof will give many years of service

Working with ladders

More accidents are caused by using ladders unwisely than by faulty equipment. Erect the ladder safely before you climb it, and move it when work is out of reach. Never lean to the side; you could lose your balance. Follow these simple, commonsense rules:

Securing the ladder

If the ground is soft, place a wide board under the feet of a ladder; screw a block across the board to hold the ladder in place. On hard ground, make sure the ladder has antislip end caps, and lay a sandbag at the base. Secure the rails with rope tied to stakes driven into the ground at each side and just behind the ladder (1).

When you extend a ladder, the sections should overlap by at least a quarter of their length. Don't lean the top of the ladder against gutters because they are slippery and, if in poor condition, may give way. Never lean a ladder against glass.

If you feel particularly uncomfortable on the ladder, you can often anchor it near the top by tying it to a heavy board held across the inside of the window frame. Make sure that the board extends about one foot on each side of the window, and pad the ends with cloth to protect the wall from damage (2).

Safety aloft

Never climb higher than four rungs from the top of the ladder; you will not be able to balance properly and there will be nothing to hold onto within easy reach. Keep both your feet on a rung, and your hips centered between the uprights. Avoid slippery footholds by placing an old towel at the foot of the ladder to dry your boots before you start climbing.

Unless the manufacturer states otherwise, don't use a ladder to form a horizontal walkway–even with a scaffold board lying on it.

Stepladders are prone to toppling sideways. On uneven surfaces, clamp a brace to one of the stiles (3).

1 Staking a ladder.
Secure the base of the ladder by tying it to stakes in the ground.

2 Securing the top.
Anchor the ladder to a board held inside the window frame.

CLAMPS

BRACE

3 Supporting a stepladder.
Clamp a brace to the rail to stabilize a stepladder.

When you buy or rent a ladder, bear in mind that:

● Wooden ladders should be made from knot-free straight-grained lumber.
● Good-quality wooden ladders have hardwood rungs tenoned through the rails (uprights).
● Wooden rungs with reinforcing metal rods stretched under them are safer than rungs without reinforcing.
● End caps or foot pads are an advantage, to prevent the ladder from slipping on hard ground.
● Choose an adjustable ladder that will give you to gain access to various parts of the building and will convert to a compact unit for storage.
● The rungs of overlapping sections of an extension ladder should align to provide a wide surface for standing.
● Choose an extension ladder with a rope and pulley, plus a latch that locks the extension to its rung.
● Choose a stepladder with a platform at the top to take paint cans and trays. This platform also helps stabilize the ladder.
● Treads should be comfortable to stand on. Wide, flat treads are best.
● Stepladders with extended rails give you a handhold at the top of the steps.

Is the ladder safe to use?

Check ladders regularly, and especially before using them after a winter's break. Inspect a rented ladder before using it. Look for splits along the rails, make sure there are no missing or broken rungs, and verify that the joints are tight. Check that the ladder is not twisted, or it could rock when leaned against a wall.

Inspect wooden ladders for rot. Even a small amount of sponginess or a few holes could signify serious damage below the surface. Test that the wood is sound before using the ladder, and treat it with a preservative. If in doubt, scrap the ladder.

Check that ladder hardware is secure. Lubricate moving hardware with oil. Inspect the pulley rope for fraying; replace it if necessary.

Regularly apply a finishing oil or varnish to wooden ladders so they don't dry out. Apply extra coats to the rungs. Don't paint a ladder. This could hide serious defects.

How to handle a ladder

Carry a ladder upright, not slung across your shoulder. Hold the ladder vertically, bend your knees slightly, then rock the ladder back against your shoulder. Grip one rung lower down while you support the ladder at head height with your other hand, and then straighten your knees.

To erect an extension ladder, lay it on the ground with its feet against the wall. Gradually raise it to vertical as you walk toward the wall. Pull the feet out from the wall so that the ladder is resting at an angle of about 70 degrees. If the ladder extends to 26 feet, for example, its feet should be 6½ feet, or a quarter of its height, from the wall.

Hold an extension ladder upright while raising it to the required height. If it is a heavy ladder, get someone to hold it while you operate the pulley.

Handling a ladder
Carry the ladder upright, leaning it back against your shoulder; grip one rung low down, another at head height.

Roof safety

Roof maintenance

Working on a roof can be hazardous. If you are unsure of yourself when working high off the ground, hire a contractor to do the work. If you decide to do it yourself, it's best not to use ladders alone for roof repairs. Rent sectional scaffolding and scaffolding boards to provide a safe working platform.

All roofing materials are fragile, to a certain extent. Masonry roofing like slate, clay, and concrete tiles can break easily. Wood shingles and shakes get brittle over time. And even common asphalt roofing can be easily damaged, especially if you walk over it on a hot sunny day when the shingles are soft.

When you combine the possibility of roof damage with the safety concerns related to working off the ground, you may think twice about working on your roof. But there are ways to do so safely without damaging the roofing. One of the best is to use a roof ladder (see below).

Roof ladders are common rental items that are made with elevated rails that keep the treads clear of the roof surface and spread the load over a larger area. The top section hooks over the ridge to keep the ladder from sliding. A roof ladder should reach from the scaffold at the eaves to the ridge of the roof. Some models are equipped with wheels, so you can roll the ladder up the slope and then turn it over to engage the hook. Never leave tools on the roof when they are not being used. Keep those that are needed inside a tool belt or a drywall bucket hanging from the side of a ladder tread.

A roof ladder allows safe access to roof

Roof coverings have a limited life, the length depending on the quality of materials used, the installation workmanship, and the exposure to severe weather. An average asphalt shingle roof can be expected to last for 20 years. But some materials, like slate and clay tiles, can last for 100 years or more. Of course, proper maintenance will always extend longevity, no matter what type of material is installed on your roof.

Replacing a roof tile

Individual tiles can be difficult to remove because of the the retaining nibs on their back edges and their interlocking shape. To remove a plain tile that is broken, lift the nibs clear of the board that it rests on, then pull the tile out. This is easier if the overlapping tiles are first raised on wood wedges inserted at both sides of the tile **(1)**. If the tile is also nailed, try rocking it loose. If this fails, you will have to break it out carefully. You may then have to use a ripper to extract or cut any remaining nails.

Use a similar technique for a single-lap interlocking tile, but in this case you will also have to wedge up the tile to the left of the one being removed **(2)**. If the tile has a deep profile, you will have to ease up a number of surrounding tiles to achieve the required clearance.

If you are removing tiles in order to install something, for example a roof vent, then you can afford to break the one you are replacing. Use a hammer to crack it, taking care not to

1 Lift the overlapping tiles with wedges

2 Lift interlocking tiles above and to the left

damage any of the adjacent tiles. The remaining tiles should be easier to remove once the first is taken out.

Installing ridge tiles

When the old mortar breaks down, a whole row of ridge tiles can be left with practically nothing but their weight holding them in place. Lift off the ridge tiles and clear all the crumbling mortar from the roof and from the undersides of the tiles. Be sure to soak the tiles in water before reinstalling them.

Mix 1 part cement and 3 parts sand to make a stiff mortar. Load a bucket about half full and carry it onto the roof. Dampen the top courses of the roof tiles or slates and lay a thick bed of mortar on each side of the ridge, following the line left behind by the old mortar **(1)**. Lay mortar for one or two tiles at a time.

Press each ridge tile firmly into the mortar, and use a trowel to slice off mortar that has squeezed out. Try not to smear any on the tile itself.

Build up a bed of mortar to fill the hollow end of each ridge tile, inserting pieces of tile or slate to prevent the mortar from slumping **(2)**. Install the rest of the tiles in the same way.

1 Apply bed of mortar on both sides of ridge

2 Insert pieces of slate to stabilize mortar

Installing new slate

Inspecting a slate roof

During the long life of a slate roof, patching can become a regular maintenance chore. But there comes a time when it simply makes more sense to start over. If you have to replace a slate roof, you're in for a big, expensive job, and any way to cut the costs is welcome.

One strategy is to remove the old slate carefully so some of it can be reused. For example, you may want new slate installed on the front side of the roof, but be willing to live with the older slate installed on the back side or on a garage roof. If the slate is carefully removed, you may also be able to sell it in bulk to roofing companies that specialize in restoration work. Reinstalling a slate roof is definitely a job for an experienced roofing contractor who has good references.

The roofs of older houses should be checked at least once a year. Start by taking a look at the roof from ground level. Usually, loose or askew slates can be spotted easily against the regular lines of the rest of the roofing. The color of any newly exposed slate will also indicate damage.

Look at the ridge against the sky to check for misalignment and gaps in the joints. Make a closer inspection with binoculars, focusing on all the flashing around chimneys, vents, and roof windows.

From inside an unfinished attic, you will be able to spot daylight through breaks in the slate. Also check the roof framing for water stains, which would indicate failure in the roofing or the flashing.

Removing and replacing a slate

1 Pull out nails

A slate may slip out of place because the nails have corroded or because the slate itself has broken. Whatever the cause, loose or broken slates should be replaced as soon as possible, before a high wind strips them off the roof.

Use a ripper to remove the trapped part of a broken slate. Slip the ripper under the slate and locate its hooked end over one of the nails **(1)**. Then pull down hard on the tool to extract or cut through the nail. Remove the second nail in the same way. Even where an old slate has already fallen out completely, you still need to remove the nails so you can install the replacement slate.

You will not be able to nail a new slate in place. Instead, use a 1-inch-wide copper strip or a plastic clip designed for holding replacement slates in place. Attach the strip to the roof by driving a nail between the slates of the lower course **(2)**, then slide the new slate into position and turn back the end of the strip to secure it **(3)**.

2 Nail strip to roof

Cutting slates and tiles

3 Fold strip over slate

Cutting slates You may have to cut a slate to fit the gap in your roof. With a sharp point, scratch a cutline on the back of the slate. Then place the slate beveled side down on a bench or sawhorse. Hold the slate so the cutline is over the edge of the work surface. Then chop the slate with the edge of a mason's trowel. You can also use a slate cutter, if you can find one to rent. It works like a pair of sheetmetal snips. Either drill nail holes or punch them out with a masonry nail. A punched hole leaves a recess for the head of a roofing nail.

Cutting cement slates Having scribed deep lines, break a cement tile over a straightedge or cut it to size with a circular saw outfitted with a masonry-cutting blade. If you saw cement slates, wear a dust mask and goggles. These slates are relatively brittle, so bore nail holes with a drill.

Cutting tiles If you need to cut roof tiles, either use an abrasive blade in a circular saw or rent an angle grinder for the purpose. Always wear protective goggles and a dust mask when cutting tile.

Cut slate with trowel

Or use slate cutter

Cutting roof tiles with an angle grinder
Follow scored guideline with cutting disc

Replacing wood shingles

Thorough ventilation is the key to preserving wood shingles. Unless they can dry out after becoming wet, they will rot. Shingle roofs often have wide spaces between decking boards to allow significant airflow underneath. However, even if a solid sheathing like plywood is used, asphalt felt underlayment should never be installed between the sheathing and the shingles. If the roof has wood shakes instead of shingles, under-layment is recommended.

When you need to repair wood shingles or shakes, your first goal is to avoid causing more damage to the roof while you're working. Old wood shingles can be very brittle. The best time for shingle repair is the day after a soaking rain, when the shingles are still soft and somewhat pliable.

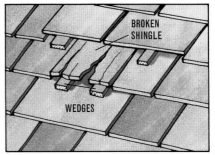
1 Using wedges
Drive wedges beneath damaged shingle and overlapping shingles in upper course.

Access

To gain good access to the top of a broken shingle, you must lift the shingles above it with small wood wedges. Carefully drive the wedges under the good shingles until there's a gap of about ¼ inch. Then drive wedges under the bottom edge of the broken shingle to lift it slightly off the roof **(1)**.

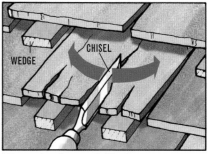
2 Removing damaged shingle
Remove damaged shingle by splitting it apart using a chisel.

Removing the shingle

Using a chisel, split the broken shingle in several places, and pull out the waste **(2)**. Split the pieces that are still held by the nails until the pieces can be pulled free.

To cut the nails, use a plain hacksaw blade with its end covered in duct tape **(3)**. Cut the nails flush with the surface of the shingle below, so the new shingle will lay flat. Remove all the dust and wood chips from the repair area.

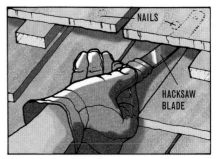
3 Sawing through nails
Saw through nails that held damaged shingle. Use a hacksaw blade wrapped with duct tape.

Installing the new shingles

Cut a new shingle to width so there's a ¼-inch gap on both sides. Then slide the shingle into the opening so its bottom edge lines up with the ones next to it. Remove the wedges that are holding up the shingles on the next course, and press these shingles down. Drive two nails into the replacement shingle. These should be located 1 inch in from both sides and 1 inch below the shingles above **(4)**.

Making ridge repairs

Traditionally the ridge on wood roofs has been covered in two ways. One is with two boards nailed over the last course of shingles and butted together above the ridge. These boards are usually 1 x 4 cedar planks. If these boards are cracked, they should be replaced.

The other ridge-sealing method uses shingles that are nailed together in pairs to form a V-shaped cap. Each cap is nailed in place along the ridge, much like an asphalt shingle ridge cap. All the nails are covered by ensuing caps, and the exposure of the cap shingles matches the exposure on the roof. Broken cap shingles are repaired in the same way as other shingles.

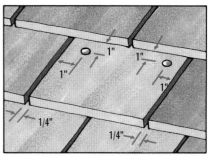
4 Installing new shingle in line with others
Leave ¼-inch gap on each side. Nail in place 1 inch from shingle edges and overlapping shingles.

Asphalt shingles

Types of asphalt shingles

Curled shingles, or those that are slightly torn or broken off, can be repaired. Badly damaged shingles should be replaced. It's a good idea to take the weather into account before starting work. Pick a warm (but not hot) day if possible, so that shingles will be pliable but not soft to the touch. Cold stiffens asphalt shingles, causing them to crack easily.

The most common type of asphalt shingles are the three-tab variety. These shingles usually measure 3 feet long and 1 foot wide. The length is divided into three sections, called tabs, that are each about 1 foot wide. Other types of asphalt shingles are available. There are strip shingles which have no tabs, interlocking shingles that hook into each other so they're less prone to wind damage, and the newer architectural shingles that have a series of overlapping tabs that are meant to simulate slate and cedar shingle roofing. When properly installed, all these shingles work well.

Repairing asphalt shingles

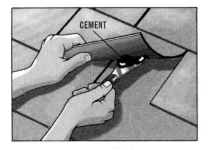

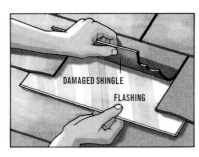

1 Fixing curled shingles
Apply a spot of roofing cement to the underside, then weigh down the shingle with a brick. For torn shingles, apply cement liberally, press shingle down, and nail both edges. Apply roofing cement to nail holes before nailing heads down.

2 Repairing broken shingles
Cut a piece of metal flashing to size of the broken shingle, plus 3 inches on both sides. Apply roofing cement to underside of flashing, slide it in place beneath damaged shingle, then apply cement to top of flashing and press damaged shingle into it.

Ridge shingles

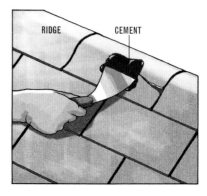

Repairing small flaws
Cover small damaged areas with roofing cement. If the damage is more extensive, repair with flashing as shown above or with a shingle patch (shown here). Apply cement to the damaged shingle, press the patch over it, and nail all four corners. Apply roofing cement to nail holes before driving the heads flush, to reduce the chance of leaks around the nails.

Replacing a shingle

1 Replacing a shingle
Carefully lift the damaged shingle and pry up the nails with a flat bar. Then lift the shingle above the damaged one, pull the nails, and remove the shingle. Stubborn nails that remain should be driven flush with a flat bar and hammer.

2 Sliding the new shingle into place
Align the bottom edge of the new shingle with the edges of the adjacent shingles. Lift up the shingles above so you can nail the new shingle in place. Apply cement to the underside of all lifted shingles, and press them flat.

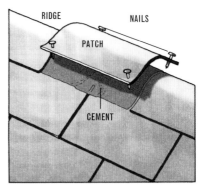

Replacing chimney flashing

Flashing

Chimney flashing is usually in two parts: the base, or step, flashing that wraps completely around the chimney and under the roofing, and the cap, or counter, flashing that covers the top of the base flashing.

To replace chimney flashing, use a cold chisel to carefully chip out the mortar joints that hold the cap flashing and remove it. Then chisel the joints deeper, to a depth of about 1½ inches. Remove any roof shingles or other covering that overlaps the base flashing, and carefully pry it free. Use the old flashing pieces as patterns to cut new pieces, preferably from copper sheet sold for the purpose. Bend the flashing to shape after cutting, then fasten it in place using roofing cement. Attach the front piece of base flashing first, then the sides. Fasten the back piece last.

Reinstall, or replace, the shingles that cover the base flashing. Then install the cap flashing in the same order as the base flashing: front, sides, back. Fill all the joints with fresh mortar, and when it is fully cured, seal the joints with roofing cement.

Flashing is used to prevent water from getting under the roofing where two or more planes of a roof meet, or where the roof meets a wall. It is also used along edges of roofs, and around windows and doors to direct water away from the inside of the house. Flashing is also required around all vent openings. Roll roofing is commonly used for some flashing, particularly along valleys where two roofs meet. But the most durable flashing materials are aluminum and copper. Both are sold in rolls and rigid pieces.

Inspecting flashing

Inspect flashing at least once a year. Look for cracks or other damage where the flashing meets the chimney **(1)**, vent stack **(2)**, wall **(3)**, and dormer **(4)**, where roof planes meet at valleys **(5)**, along the rakes **(6)** and eaves **(7)**, and over the windows **(8)** and the doors **(9)**.

Very old flashing sometimes develops pinholes which are hard to see. These can be repaired by coating them with plastic roof cement.

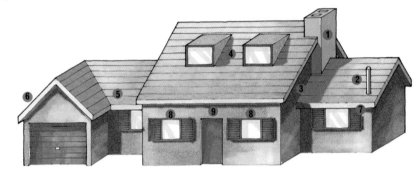

Maintenance and repair

It is not a bad idea to coat all flashing seams periodically with plastic roofing cement, especially at chimneys and around vent stacks. Apply the cement using a small mason's trowel and smooth the surface of the cement so that it does not form hollows and ridges where water may collect. Where you find holes 1-square-inch or bigger, cut a patch from the same material as the flashing. Make it 1 inch larger than the hole all around. Apply cement to the damaged flashing, press the patch into place, then cover the entire area with cement and smooth the surface.

Repointing flashing

Where flashing meets brick, it is usually embedded in mortar. Separations here require immediate repair since the loose flashing actually collects water and funnels it between the bricks where it can spread and do considerable damage. If the flashing itself is sound, just rake out the old mortar from the joint to a depth of about ¾ inch. Press the flashing back into place, wedging it if necessary with small stones. Then, using a trowel, fill the seam with fresh mortar. Smooth the joint carefully. After the mortar has fully cured, seal the flashing with roofing cement.

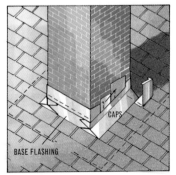

Rake out joint and repoint with fresh mortar.

Galvanic action

Dissimilar metals touching each other react when wet. As a result, metal flashing must be fastened with nails made of the same metal as the flashing, otherwise one or the other will corrode, often quickly. If it is impossible to match flashing and fasteners, use neoprene washers to prevent direct contact between the two metals. The chart (right) shows common construction metals. When paired, metals farthest apart in the chart corrode soonest and fastest. Metals in contact with acidic woods, like redwood and cedar, can also corrode.

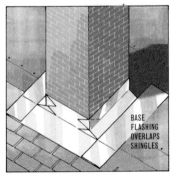

Base flashing

BASE FLASHING OVERLAPS SHINGLES.

Cap flashing

CAPS

BASE FLASHING

Corrosion Table
1 Aluminum
2 Zinc
3 Steel
4 Tin
5 Lead
6 Brass
7 Copper
8 Bronze

Flashing repairs

Vertical wall flashing

Individual, overlapping flashing shingles are often installed where dormers join roofs and where a roof joins a higher wall. To locate and repair leaks in these areas, the siding and roofing must be removed.

Look for rotten or discolored sheathing, and evidence that settling has occurred, which may have pulled house sections apart slightly. After repairing the problems, fill gaps between building sections with strips of wood. Apply new felt underlayment over the wood, then reflash the area as you reshingle.

To do this, attach a flashing shingle at the end of each course, fastened to the vertical surface with one nail at the upper corner. Each flashing shingle should overlap the one underneath, and extend at least 4 inches up the adjacent wall and 2 inches under the roofing. After the flashing and the roofing are completely installed, attach new siding to cover the top edge of the flashing.

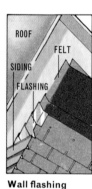

Wall flashing

Drip flashing

During construction, strips of flashing are installed above doors and windows and along the edges of the roof. These should extend several inches under the siding or roof covering and be nailed well away from the edges. On roofs, the drip edge goes on top of the underlayment along the rake and beneath it at the eaves. If minor repairs do not suffice, remove the siding or roof covering that overlaps the flashing. Determine the cause of the leak, then replace the drip edge, cover any seams with roofing cement, and reinstall the siding or roofing material.

Drip edge

Flat roof flashing

Layers of felt that constitute a built-up roof are generally left long at the edges to create a raised flashing that angles up to adjacent walls. Cracks often develop where the turn begins. To repair, first cement down any loose roofing, then cover the area with a generous layer of roofing cement. Cut additional strips of felt, and build up the flashing by laying down alternate layers of felt and cement to obtain a smooth, even rise with no hollows that can retain water.

Flat roof

Flashing a vent stack

Sometimes you may be able to stop leaks by tightening the lead collar (if one is present) around the neck of a pipe where it passes through the roof.

To do this, tap the collar with a blunt cold chisel and a hammer. Work around the upper rim of the collar, sealing it against the stack.

Also try coating the entire flashing area and lower portion of the vent stack with roofing cement. If a good repair is not possible, then you'll have to install new flashing.

First, carefully remove the shingles that are covering the old flashing. In some cases you can just slip a new piece of flashing over the old one and replace the roofing.

But in most cases, you'll have to pry up the old flashing **(1)**, place a new piece of felt on the the roof sheathing, install the new flashing **(2)**, and then reinstall the roofing. The flashing should always overlap the bottom shingles and fit under the top shingles **(3)**.

1 Remove shingles and old flashing

2 Install new felt and flashing

3 Reapply shingles

Renewing valley flashing

Where shingles are trimmed so that flashing is visible, the construction is called an open valley. When the shingles overlap the flashing, it's called a closed valley.

Small repairs to open valley flashing can be made with roofing cement. Larger holes can be patched with flashing material coated on the bottom and top with roofing cement. Leaks from no apparent source may sometimes be stopped by applying a bead of cement between the edges of the trimmed shingles and the flashing.

To repair closed valley flashing, first try slipping squares of copper or aluminum flashing material underneath the shingles in the damaged area. Loosen or remove the nails closest to the valley, then bend and install the squares beginning at the bottom of the roof. Overlap them until they extend 2 inches beyond the damaged area. Renail the shingles and cover the nailheads with roofing cement. If leaks persist, remove the valley shingles and install new flashing. Then replace the shingles.

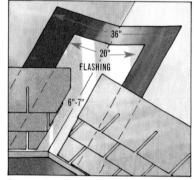

Open valley flashing

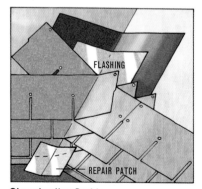

Closed valley flashing

Gutters

A properly sized system of gutters and downspouts, in good working condition, constitutes basic preventive maintenance. Gutters prevent water from running down the sides of the house, causing damage and discoloration. Combined with downspouts, gutters also direct water away from the foundation of the building, lessening the risk of the basement flooding and the foundation settling. Gutters also protect flowerbeds and other landscaping around the perimeter of the house. Inspect gutters frequently.

Gutters and downspouts

Gutters are made of a number of materials. Traditional preferences were for wood or copper. Although both are still used occasionally, most gutters now are made of galvanized steel, aluminum, and vinyl.

The size and layout of a gutter system must allow it to discharge all the water from the roof area it serves. The flow load required depends mainly on the area of the roof.

For roofs with areas less than 750 square feet, 4-inch-wide gutters usually suffice. Choose 5-inch gutters for roofs with areas between 750 and 1400 square feet. Six-inch gutters are available for even larger roofs.

Downspouts also should be properly sized to carry away runoff. For roof areas up to 1000 square feet, 3-inch downspouts are usually sufficient. Larger roofs require 4-inch downspouts.

The location of downspouts can affect the system's performance. A central downspout can serve double the roof area of one with an end outlet. A right-angled bend in guttering will reduce the flow capacity by about 20 percent, if it is placed near the outlet downspout.

There are three basic types of hanging hardware for gutters (see below). Although 30-inch spacing is standard, 24-inch spacing provides better support to withstand snow and ice loads.

Gutter spike is driven through gutter into fascia board. Sleeve fits in trough.

Strap hanger fastens under shingle

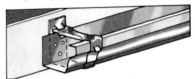

Bracket fastens to fascia board

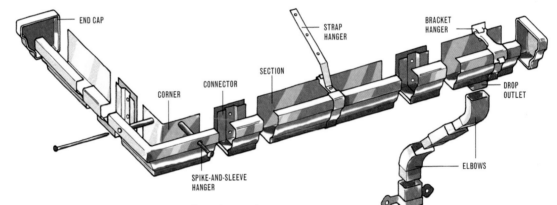

Gutter materials

Wood gutters, made of fir, redwood, or red cedar, are all decay resistant. Generally they are used with wood-shingled roofs. Wood gutters are very sturdy and if maintained will last the life of the house.

Galvanized steel gutters are often the lowest priced of all systems. Available unfinished or enameled, they have a short life compared to other materials unless frequently repainted. Paint does not adhere well to galvanized steel unless a special primer is used to prevent the new paint from flaking.

Aluminum is a very common gutter material. Available in several enamel colors, it is lightweight and corrosion resistant. However, aluminum gutters will not withstand much ladder pressure. Sometimes aluminum gutters are formed in a continuous piece on site. But more often the systems are assembled in place, using stock components that are available in standard dimensions.

Vinyl gutters are becoming more popular with each passing year. Like aluminum systems, the gutter sections and fittings come in different colors and in standard sizes. Many do-it-yourselfers find them easier to install and repair than other systems.

45

Gutter maintenance

Removing debris

Repairing small holes

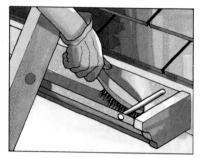

1 To repair pinholes and small rust spots
First clean the gutter and scrub the damaged area using wire brush or coarse abrasive paper. Wipe away residue using a rag dipped in paint thinner.

2 Apply coat of roofing cement
On holes larger than 1/4 inch, sandwich layers of heavy aluminum foil between coats of roofing cement. Smooth topcoat so water won't collect.

Patching large areas

CARDBOARD

1 To repair a large hole
First use thin cardboard to make a pattern, then cut a patch of the same material as the gutter to fit over the area, overlapping the hole at least 1 inch.

2 Coat with roofing cement
Press the patch into a bed of roofing cement, then crimp it over the edge of the gutter. Apply another layer of cement, smoothing it so water won't collect.

Maintaining wood gutters

Repaint wood gutters at least once every three years. Be sure to work during a period of warm, fair weather.

First clear the gutter and allow a few days for the wood to dry thoroughly. Next, sand the interior of the gutter smooth and remove the residue with a whisk broom and handheld vacuum. Wipe the sanded trough with paint thinner, then apply a thin coat of roofing cement mixed with paint thinner to brushing consistency. This helps the cement enter the pores of the wood.

After the first coat of cement has dried, wait two days, then apply a second thin coat. Sand and repaint the gutter exterior with two coats of high-quality house paint.

Snow and ice

Dislodge snow and ice buildup with a broom from an upstairs window—if you can reach it safely. Otherwise, use a ladder. If snow and ice become a regular seasonal problem, screw a snow board to the roof. Make it out of 1 x 3 treated lumber. Install it about 1 inch above the eaves, using steel straps (right).

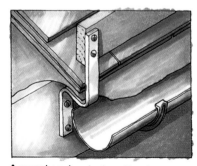

A snow board protects gutters from snow and ice

Inspect and clean out the interiors of gutters at least twice a year, in autumn after the leaves have fallen and again in early spring. Check more often if you live in a heavily wooded area. Use a ladder to reach the gutter. At least 12 inches of the ladder should extend above the gutter to provide safe working conditions.

First block the gutter outlet with a rag. Then, wearing heavy work gloves to avoid cuts, remove debris from the gutters. Scrape accumulated silt into a heap using a shaped piece of plastic or light sheetmetal. Then scoop it out with a garden trowel and deposit it in a bucket hung from the ladder.

Sweep the gutter clean with a whisk broom, then remove the rag and flush the gutter using a garden hose. Check whether the water drains completely or remains in standing pools, indicating a sagging gutter section.

Leaking seams where gutter sections are joined can be sealed using silicone caulk. For the best seal, disassemble the sections, apply caulk inside the seam, then reassemble the joint. Otherwise, spread caulk over the seam on the inside of the gutter and smooth the surface to avoid producing ridges that might trap water.

If downspouts are clogged, free them using a plumber's snake or drain auger. Work from the bottom if possible, to avoid compacting debris further. If necessary, disassemble the downspout sections to get at the blockage.

If downspout blockages are frequent, install leaf strainers in the gutter outlets. Or in severe situations, attach wire-mesh leaf guards over the entire length of the gutters to slow the accumulation of debris.

Leaf strainer

Wire-mesh leaf guard

Insulation & Ventilation

Insulating your home

No matter what fuel you use, the cost of heating a home continues to rise, and shows no signs of stopping. So it makes good sense to do what you can to reduce your heating bills. Turning down the thermostat is one strategy, albeit a chilly one. But this doesn't attack the problem at its source, which is usually poor (or no) insulation.

Specifications

Homes in nearly all parts of the United States benefit from some amount of insulation. Even in the warmest parts of the country, insulation is valuable in keeping excessive heat from infiltrating living spaces. It can also improve the efficiency of air conditioners by preventing cooled air from rapidly escaping. Reputable insulation contractors or your local building inspector can tell you the amount of insulation recommended for your region. When comparing thermal insulating materials, you'll be faced with these technical specifications:

U-values The building materials that are already present in your house have been rated by the construction industry and government housing authorities according to the way the materials conduct heat. For individual materials, these ratings are called K-values and represent the total heat transmitted (per square foot, per hour) between the surfaces of two materials when there is a temperature difference between the two of 1°F. When the passage of heat is measured through an entire structure (such as a wall, ceiling, or floor), which is made up of several different materials plus air spaces, the rating is called the U-value. The higher the U-value, the more rapidly heat passes from one surface of the structure to another.

R-values Adding insulation reduces U-values (but not K-values) by resisting the passage of heat through a structure. The degree of resistance is termed the R-value. Insulation is compared and sold by this rating. Materials with superior insulating qualities have the highest R-values.

Deciding on your priorities

For many people, the initial expense of total house insulation is prohibitive, even though they may concede that it is cost-effective in the long term. Nevertheless, it's important to begin insulating as soon as you can, because every measure you take contributes some savings.

Many authorities suggest that in an average house, 35 percent of lost heat escapes through the walls, 25 percent through the roof, 25 percent through drafty doors and windows, and 15 percent through the floor. At best, this is no more than a rough guide, as it is difficult to define an "average" home in order to estimate the rate of heat loss. A town house, for example, will lose less than a detached house of identical size, even though their roofs have the same area and are in similar condition. And other factors are relevant, too—for instance, large, ill-fitting, double-hung windows permit far greater heat loss than small, tightly fitting casements.

Although these statistics identify the major routes for heat loss, they don't necessarily indicate where you should begin your insulation program in order to achieve the quickest return on your investment or, for that matter, the most immediate improvement in terms of comfort. In fact, it is best to start with relatively inexpensive measures.

1 Water heater and pipes Begin by insulating your water-heater tank and any exposed pipes running through unheated areas of your house. This improvement will result in noticeable savings in just a few months.

2 Radiators Attach aluminum foil to the walls behind your radiators. The foil will reflect heat into the room before the wall absorbs it.

3 Weather stripping Seal off air leaks around windows and doors with weather-stripping materials. For a modest expense, weather stripping provides a substantial return economically and in terms of your comfort. It's also easy to install.

4 Roof Tackle the insulation of your roof next, because it's usually considered the most cost-effective major insulating job. It not only reduces fuel bills, but can make you eligible for utility company rebates or credits.

5 Walls Depending on the construction of your house, insulating the walls may be a sound investment. However, it's likely to be expensive and it will be several years (if not more) before you recoup your initial investment.

6 Floors Most floors are insulated to a certain degree by carpet and rugs. But, adding insulation between the floor joists is not usually cost-effective. Let your comfort be the deciding factor. If a floor is too cold with carpet and rugs in place, then consider adding some insulation.

7 Storm windows Contrary to typical advertisements, storm windows produce a slow return on your investment. However, they do help increase the value of your home, make your rooms less drafty, and cut down on some of the noise coming from outside. Installing new windows instead of new storms is a better idea when it comes to energy conservation, but it can be very expensive.

Pipes, water heaters, and radiators

Insulating a water heater

One of the least expensive and most effective energy-saving projects is to insulate your water heater. Even so-called insulated heaters rarely have more than 1 inch of insulation surrounding the tank. Many hardware stores, home centers, and heating supply outlets sell commercial kits containing precut fiberglass insulation for wrapping around the outside of many different size tanks. These kits are normally inexpensive and perform so well that it's worth taking some time to find one.

If you can't find one for your heater, make one. Just cut some strips of paper-faced fiberglass insulation (the thicker the better) with a sharp utility knife. Then wrap the strips horizontally around the tank, beginning at the bottom. Joint the strips at the seams with duct tape.

Be sure to leave the thermostat, temperature-and-pressure (T&P) relief valve, and any control knobs exposed so you'll have easy access later for servicing the tank. And when working on gas- or oil-fired heaters, cut the insulation to stop within 2 inches of the vent stack at the top of the tank and 2 inches from the air-intake holes at the bottom of the tank. These should be exposed to prevent fire and to make sure the tank performs properly.

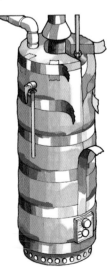

Insulating a hot-water cylinder
Fit insulation snugly around the cylinder and wrap pipe insulation around the pipework.

Insulating pipes

You should insulate hot-water pipes in those parts of the house where their radiant heat is not contributing to the warmth of the rooms, and cold-water pipes in unheated areas of the building, where they could freeze. The best way to insulate these pipes is with foam pipe insulation, designed just for this job.

This insulation comes in tube form, and is produced to fit pipes of different diameters. Usually it's available in ½-inch and ¾-inch diameter, and sometimes you'll have the option of ½- or ¾-inch-thick tube walls. The thicker tubes, of course, provide more insulation. Some tubes incorporate a metallic foil backing that reflects some of the heat back into hot-water pipes.

Most tubes are preslit along their length so that they can be stretched over the pipe **(1)**. Butt each successive length against the one before, end to end, and seal the joints with tape.

At a bend, cut small segments out of the split edge so that it bends without crimping. Fit it around the pipe **(2)** and seal the closed joints with tape. Cover a 90-degree elbow with two mitered pipes. Just cut the ends with a utility knife, slide the pieces together **(3)**, and seal with tape. Cut lengths of tube to fit snugly around a T-joint, using a wedge-shaped butt joint **(4)**, and seal with tape as before.

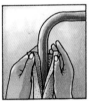

1 Stretch onto pipe **2 Cut to fit bend** **3 Miter over elbows** **4 Butt at T-joints**

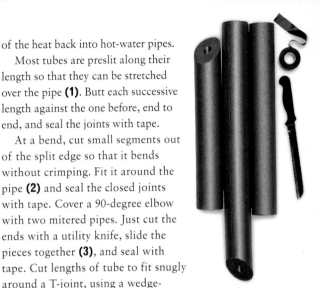

Foam pipe insulation
This type of insulation is lightweight and easy to work with. You can cut it with a utility knife or scissors and join it with tape.

Reflecting heat from a radiator

As much as 25 percent of the radiant heat from a radiator can be lost to the wall behind it. You can reclaim as much as half of this wasted heat by applying aluminum foil or a foil-faced polystyrene panel to the wall behind the radiator. Both will reflect the heat back into the room, but the panel is the more durable option. The material is usually available in sheets and is easiest to apply when the radiator has been moved for other remodeling work. But, you can do it with the radiator in place.

Turn off the radiator and measure it and the location of any wall-mounted brackets. Use a sharp utility knife or scissors to cut the sheet to to size. For the best appearance, make it slightly smaller than the radiator all around. Cut narrow slots to fit over any brackets **(1)**.

Apply wallpaper paste to the back of the material, then slide it behind the radiator **(2)**. Smooth it onto the wall and allow the paste to dry before turning on the radiator. You can also used double-sided tape to hold it in place.

1 Cut slots to align with wall brackets

2 Slide lining behind radiator and press to wall

Draftproofing doors

A certain amount of ventilation is desirable to maintain good indoor air quality and to keep condensation at bay. However, allowing uncontrolled drafts is hardly an efficient way to ventilate a house. Drafts account for a large amount of heat loss in any house, and are also responsible for a good deal of discomfort. Adding threshold seals is the best way to combat substantial door drafts. These devices are easy to install, require no special tools or knowledge, and are available in many different shapes and sizes.

Flexible strip

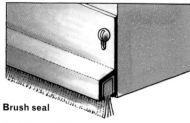

Brush seal

Spring hinge

Flexible arch

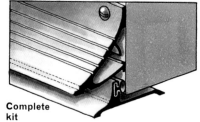

Complete kit

Locating and curing drafts

Tackle the exterior doors first. Then turn your attention to interior doors and seal only those that border unheated rooms—for example, a door from the kitchen to a mudroom, or one from a hallway to an unused bedroom or to the attic stairs.

Locate drafts by running the flat of your hand along the bottom of the door. If you dampen your skin, it will enhance its sensitivity to cold. Otherwise, wait for a very windy day in order to conduct your search.

Threshold sealing devices are made by many different manufacturers, and there are so many variations that it's impossible to describe every type here. But the following examples illustrate the principles that are commonly used to seal out drafts.

Threshold seals

The gap between the bottom of an exterior door and the floor can be very large and, if not properly sealed, can admit fierce drafts, especially on the coldest days. To close this opening, install a threshold seal. Buy one that fits the opening exactly if possible. Otherwise, buy the next bigger size and cut it to fit your door.

Flexible-strip seals The simplest form of threshold seal is a flexible strip of plastic or rubber that sweeps against the floor-covering to close the gap. The most basic versions are simply self-adhesive strips. Other types have a rigid plastic or aluminum extrusion that is screwed to the face of the door. This securely holds the sealing strip in contact with the floor.

Flexible-strip seals are inexpensive and easy to install. But they tend to wear out quickly. They work best over smooth flooring.

Brush seals A long nylon-bristle brush, set into a metal or plastic extrusion, can be used to exclude draft under doors. This kind of threshold seal is suitable for slightly uneven floors and textured floorcoverings. It is the only type that can be fitted to sliding doors as well as hinged ones.

Spring-hinge seals This seal has a plastic strip and extruded clip that are spring-loaded, so they lift from the floor as the door is opened. When you close the door, the seal is pressed against the floor by a stop screwed to the doorframe. Suitable for both interior and exterior doors, these seals operate silently and inflict little wear on floorcoverings. They are also ideal for uneven floors.

Flexible-arch seals This type of seal consists of an arched vinyl insert, fitted to a shallow aluminum extrusion, that presses against the bottom edge of the door. Because it has to be nailed or screwed to the floor, a flexible-arch excluder is difficult to use on a solid concrete floor. For an external door, choose a version that has additional underseal to prevent rain from seeping beneath it. To install it, you may have to plane the bottom edge of the door.

Door kits The best solution for an exterior door is to buy a kit combining an aluminum weather trim, which is designed to shed rain-water, and a weather bar fitted with a tubular seal that's made of rubber or plastic. The trim is screwed to the face of the door, and the weather bar is screwed to the threshold.

Weather-stripping doors

Sealing gaps around the door

Any well-fitting door needs a 1/16-inch gap at the top and sides so that it can operate smoothly. However, a gap this large can let a great deal of heat escape. There are several ways to seal these gaps, some of which are described here. The cheaper versions have to be replaced regularly.

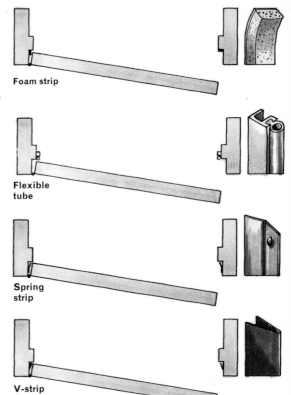

Foam strip

Flexible tube

Spring strip

V-strip

Weather stripping
Flexible foam and vinyl strips are easy to cut and apply

Foam weather stripping The most straightforward seal is a self-adhesive foam strip, which you stick around the doorjamb next to the stop. The strip is compressed when the door is closed, forming a seal. The cheapest polyurethane foam will be good for one or two seasons (although it's useless if painted) and is suitable for interior doors only. The better-quality vinyl-coated polyurethane, rubber, or PVC foams are more durable. When applying foam strips, avoid stretching them, because this reduces their effectiveness. The door may be difficult to close at first, but the strip will compress slightly over time and the door will work better.

Flexible-tube weather stripping A small vinyl tube, held in a plastic or metal extrusion, is compressed to fill the gap around the door. The cheapest versions have a flange that can be nailed or stapled to the doorstop.

Spring strips These thin metal or plastic strips have a sprung leaf that is either nailed or glued to the doorjamb. The top and closing edges of the door brush past the sprung leaf, sealing the gap. The hinged edge simply compresses the leaf on that side of the door. This type of strip does not work well on uneven surfaces unless the leaf comes with a foam strip glued in place.

V-strips This design is a variation on the spring strip: The leaf is bent back to form a V-shape. The strip is mounted on the jamb to fill the gap around the door. These products are inexpensive and easy to install.

Sealing keyholes and mail slots

An external keyhole should be fitted with a coverplate to keep out drafts during the winter. You can buy a hinged flap that screws onto the inside of the door to cover a mail slot. The best ones have a brush seal behind the flap.

Keyhole coverplate
The coverplate is part of the escutcheon

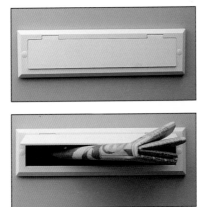

Brush seal
An integral brush seal prevents drafts from entering when the flap is open.

Window weather stripping

Sealing hinged casement windows is straightforward. You can use most of the options suggested for doors (see previous page). But weather-stripping a double-hung window is a bit more complicated, because there are more mating surfaces.

Double-hung windows

The top and bottom rails of a double-hung window can be sealed with any type of compressible weather stripping. The sliding edges admit fewer drafts, but they can be sealed with a brush seal fixed to the frame. Mount it on the inside for the lower sash, on the outside for the top one. To seal the gap between the central meeting rails, use a V-strip or a compressible strip. For square faces, use a blade-seal strip.

1 Brush seal

2 V-strip

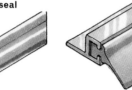

3 Compressible strip   **4 Blade seal**

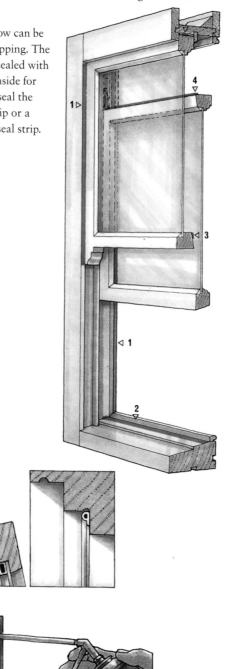

Sealing a pivoting window

When you close a pivoting window, the movable frame comes to rest against fixed stops. Adding weather stripping to these stops will seal off the worst drafts. You can use compressible strips, V-strips, or high-quality flexible tubes for this job. Just make sure you pick products that are weatherproof.

Flexible-tube seal for a pivot window

Filling large gaps

Large gaps left around newly installed windows (or doors) are often a source of big drafts. The same is true of holes drilled through the walls for vents and electrical services. Use an expanding-foam filler to seal these gaps. Once the filler has set, trim it flush with the surrounding surfaces.

Seal large gaps with expanding foam

Floors and baseboards

A ventilated crawlspace below a first-floor room can be the source of significant drafts, through gaps either in the floorboards or underneath the baseboard. The best way to seal the floorboards is to install fiberglass insulation between the joists. To seal the gap between the baseboard and the floor, fill it with caulk and then cover the caulked area with shoe molding for a clean appearance.

Seal gap with mastic and wooden quadrant

Attic access panels

Newer houses don't always have big attics that are accessible from stairs. Too often the roof is made with trusses instead of rafters, so there isn't much usable space to justify easy access. Instead, attic access is provided by a panel that covers an opening in the ceiling, usually in a closet or hall.

Some attics have fold-down staircases that are nothing more than ladders. In this case the ceiling panel is hinged, and when you pull it down, the ladder unfolds and rests on the floor.

To reduce drafts from an attic stairway door, weather-strip the door (page 51). Sealing access panels or fold-down stairs requires adding weather stripping to the framing that the panels rest against.

Drafty fireplaces

A chimney can be an annoying source of drafts. If you want to retain the look of an open fireplace, cut a sheet of thick polystyrene to seal the flue of the chimney, but leave a hole about 2 inches across to provide some ventilation. When you want to use the fireplace again, don't forget to remove the polystyrene—it's flammable.

Insulating roofs

Approximately a quarter of the heat lost from an average house goes through the roof, so minimizing this should be one of your top priorities. Usually, insulating your roof means insulating the ceiling just below the roof. To do this, you just add insulation between the ceiling joists. But if you want to convert your attic into living space, now or in the future, it makes sense to insulate between the rafters. This is harder to do, but it stops heat loss and it gives extra living space.

Preparing the attic

On inspection, you may find that the ceiling under your roof already has insulation, just not enough of it. At one time even an inch of insulation was considered to be acceptable. It's worth installing extra insulation to bring it up to the recommended minimum R-value rating for your region. Also, check the roof framing for signs of rot or roof leaks so they can be treated before you begin.

Remember that the plaster or drywall ceiling below will not support your weight. When working in the attic, lay several planks across the joists so you can move about safely.

If you don't have a light fixture in the attic, now is a good time to install one. But if you don't want to go through the trouble, just run an extension cord with a work light on the end into the attic and hang it high up to provide overall light.

Most attics are very dusty, so wear old clothes (long sleeves and long pants) and a dust mask. Also, wear gloves and safety glasses, especially if you're handling fiberglass insulation, which irritates the skin.

Types of roof insulation

There's a wide range of insulating materials available, so it is important to check the recommended types for your area with the local building code authorities.

Blanket insulation Fiberglass and mineral- or rock-wool blanket insulation is commonly sold as rolls, sized in widths to fit snuggly between joists and rafters. The most common width is 16 inches, because this is the normal joist spacing. The label on the roll tells how many square feet it covers. The same material, usually cut into 4-foot lengths, is sold as "batts." A minimum thickness of 10 inches (for cold climates) and 8 inches (for warm climates) is recommended for attic insulation.

Blanket insulation is sold in three ways: unfaced, paper-faced, and foil-faced. The unfaced type is usually used for laying on attic floors where existing insulation with a vapor barrier is already in place, so a second vapor barrier should not be used.

The paper-faced product has a vapor barrier built into the facing. It is used when there is no other insulation present and a vapor barrier is required. The vapor barrier should always be installed against the warm surface; in the case of an attic, this means at the bottom of the joist space next to the plaster or drywall on the ceiling below.

The foil-faced product is used in the same way as the paper-faced product. In addition to acting as a vapor barrier, its facing is covered with foil that reflects some of the radiant heat back into the room.

Loose-fill insulation Loose-fill insulation, in pellet or granular form, is poured between the joists, up to the recommended depth. Exfoliated vermiculite, made from a mineral called mica, is the most common form. But others, like mineral-wool and polystyrene granules, are also available.

Loose fill is sold in bags that generally cover 25 square feet to a depth of 4 inches. This product works best on jobs where the joist spacing is irregular. It should not be used in very drafty attics where the material can blow about easily.

Blown insulation This insulation is installed by contractors who blow fiberglass, mineral wool, or cellulose fibers into the attic. It's very effective in old houses where joist spacing is not consistent.

Rigid insulation Boards made of dense foam, either polystyrene or polyurethane, are very efficient insulators. Most lumber yards stock them in 4 x 8 sheets, in thicknesses that range from ¾ inch to 2 inches. The boards are simply nailed to framing members and are usually used in new construction.

Vapor barriers

Installing insulation makes the attic colder than before, which increases the risk of condensation either on the framing members or within the insulation itself. In time, this could cause serious rot problems and significantly reduce the effectiveness of the insulation. When insulation is wet, it functions more like a conductor than an insulator.

One way to reduce this condensation is to provide adequate attic ventilation.

Another solution is to install a vapor barrier on the warm side of the insulation. This prevents moisture-laden house air from passing through the ceiling and into the attic. A vapor barrier is often bonded directly to the insulation. In new construction, it tends to be a separate polyethylene sheet. This type is stapled to the framing members underneath the insulation before the drywall is installed. All vapor barriers should be continuous and undamaged.

● **Ventilating the attic**
Laying insulation between the joists increases the risk of condensation in an unheated roof space. To keep the attic dry, make sure there are adequate roof, soffit, gable, or ridge vents to keep the air circulating properly.

Insulating the attic

Chimneys and pipes

Blanket insulation

Before laying blanket insulation, use flexible caulk to seal gaps around incoming pipes, vents, or wiring.

Remove the blanket's wrapping in the attic (since the insulation comes compressed, but swells to its true thickness on being released) and begin by placing one end of a roll into the eaves, vapor-barrier side down. Make sure you don't cover any soffit vents in the eaves. On a shallow-pitch roof, it's a good idea to trim the end of each blanket to a wedge shape so that it doesn't obstruct the airflow.

Unroll the blanket between the joists, pressing it down to form a snug fit—but don't compress it. Continue filling between the joists until the first layer is complete. Just

butt the leading end of the new roll tightly against the last blanket. Cut any blankets that are too wide for the space with a utility knife.

Most attics are not easy to work in. Do the best you can, and remember that the tighter the insulation blankets fit against the framing and each other, the more money you'll save on fuel costs in the future.

Don't cover with insulation any exhaust-fan housings or lighting fixtures that may protrude into the attic. Leave at least 3 inches of clearance around them to keep the insulation from overheating. Or, replace the fixtures with ones designed for direct contact with insulation.

Loose-fill insulation

Loose-fill insulation doesn't come with a vapor barrier. If there is already insulation with a vapor barrier in place, you can just spread the loose fill over it. But if there is no barrier, one must be installed before adding any loose-fill insulation. Take special care not to cover the soffit vents. To avoid blockages, wedge strips of plywood or thick cardboard between the joists so an open air passage to the soffit vents is maintained.

Pour the insulation between the joists and distribute it roughly with a broom. Level it with a piece of

hardboard about 2 feet wide.

If you want to achieve a higher R-value than you'd get with the insulation level with the top of the joists, just add more. Start at the perimeter of the room, or at the point farthest from the access hole or stairway, and pour more insulation above the joists. Work backward toward the attic access so you'll be able to get out without crawling through the insulation. Once the extra insulation is added, you won't be able to use the attic floor for storage.

Insulating around chimneys

To avoid a fire hazard, the wood framing around a chimney should be installed so it is at least 2 inches from the chimney on all sides. To insulate this area, it's best to use fiberglass batts. Just remove the facing from the insulation and loosely stuff the insulation into the spaces around the chimney. Don't pack it too tightly. If the fibers don't have some loft, their effectiveness is significantly reduced.

Insulating pipes

If you live in a cold climate and there are water pipes running between the joists, prevent them from freezing by laying blanket insulation over them. In areas where this isn't practical, insulate each pipe separately with pipe-insulating tubes.

You can also use loose-fill insulation to protect pipes. Before pouring the loose fill over them, lay a bridge made from cardboard over the pipes. This will tend to trap some of the heat coming up from the room below and prevent the pipes from freezing.

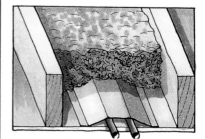

Insulating pipes between joists

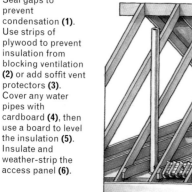

Double layers of insulation
If you want to install more than a single layer of insulation—to achieve a much higher R-value—lay the second layer at right angles to the first one.

Laying blanket insulation (right). Seal all gaps around pipes, vents, and wiring **(1)**. Place end of roll against eaves, and trim ends **(2)** or add soffit vent protectors **(3)**. Press rolls between joists **(4)**.

Spreading loose-fill insulation (far right). Seal gaps to prevent condensation **(1)**. Use strips of plywood to prevent insulation from blocking ventilation **(2)** or add soffit vent protectors **(3)**. Cover any water pipes with cardboard **(4)**, then use a board to level the insulation **(5)**. Insulate and weather-strip the access panel **(6)**.

Laying blanket insulation

Spreading loose-fill insulation

Generally, when you make an attic space into living space, you end up adding short walls under the rafters. The space where the rafters meet the floor is considered unusable, and these walls help define the space better.

Blankets or batts are usually the best choice. They're economical and easy to install. And, because there is plenty of ventilation behind the wall, you can fill the stud spaces completely with insulation. Faced insulation has an integral vapor barrier. Unfaced insulation doesn't; it needs a polyethylene vapor barrier over it.

Insulating between the rafters

If you plan to use your attic for living space, you will need to insulate between the roof rafters instead of the floor joists. Before starting, check for any roof leaks and make sure any necessary repairs are done.

Condensation is another source of trouble that must be considered before starting work. Because the roof surface will be colder after installing insulation, the likelihood of condensation increases. To eliminate condensation, you have to provide two things.

The first is proper ventilation. You should maintain a gap of at least 1½ inches between the top of the insulation and the bottom of the roof sheathing. (Because this gap is necessary, the depth between the rafters that's available for insulation is reduced. To add more insulation and still maintain the proper minimum ventilation gap, you'll have to add strips to the bottom of the rafters to create extra depth.) You also need continuous soffit vents on all eaves, and a continuous ridge vent along the top of the roof.

Second is a vapor barrier on the warm side of the insulation. You can use blankets with an integral vapor barrier, or install unfaced blankets between the rafters and staple a polyethylene sheet to the lower edges of the rafters to act as a vapor barrier. After installing the insulation, you can cover the rafters with sheets of drywall, tongue-and-groove boards, or sheets of 4 x 8 plywood paneling.

Installing blanket insulation

Cut a faced blanket to length, then lift it up and push it between the rafters. Unfold the side flanges on the facing and staple them to the undersides of the rafters. Be sure to overlap the edges on successive blankets.

Installing insulation boards

You can also use rigid polystyrene boards to insulate between rafters. To keep the boards properly aligned, and to maintain the ventilation gap above them, nail furring to the sides of the rafters. Then cut the boards for a tight fit and push them up against the furring. Cover the insulation with a polyethylene-sheet vapor barrier.

● **Where space is tight**
It is usually difficult to install enough insulation to achieve high R-values between standard-size rafters. Once you allow for a 1½-inch ventilation gap above the insulation, there's not much room left. Your options are to increase the depth of the rafters by nailing boards to the bottom edges, or to install polystyrene insulation between rafters, because it has a higher R-value per inch.

Insulating an attic from the inside.
Fit either blanket or board insulation between the rafters.
1 Minimum gap of 1½ inches between insulation and roof sheathing for ventilation.
2 Blanket or batt.
3 Vapor barrier stapled to rafters.
4 Board insulation wedged between rafters.
5 Drywall nailed over vapor barrier.
6 Roofing felt.
7 Roofing.

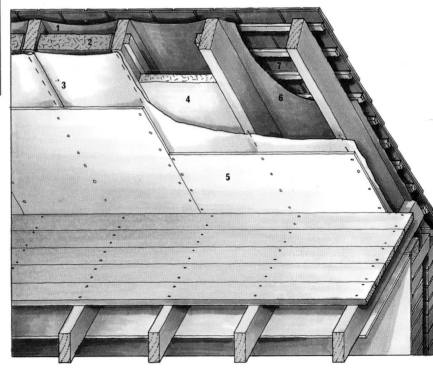

Insulating a room in the attic. Surround the room itself with insulation, but leave the floor uninsulated so the attic will benefit from heat rising from the rooms directly below.

Insulating flat roofs

Insulation options for walls

Flat roofs don't have the virtue of shedding water quickly, as pitched roofs do. Because of this, they need an elaborate roofing system that is almost always contractor-installed. If you're having a flat roof redone and you have no insulation between the rafters below, it's a good time to add insulation to the roof.

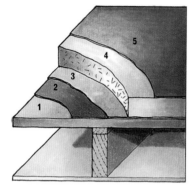

Insulating a flat roof.
Expert contractors can insulate the roof from above.

1 Roof deck
2 Waterproof covering
3 New vapor barrier
4 Insulation
5 New waterproof covering

Hot roof system

Discuss this with the contractor and sort out the options you have.

There are several different approaches to waterproofing a flat roof. One of the most common is to apply multiple layers of waterproof roofing materials. To do this, contractors usually start by stripping off all the old roofing down to the roof deck. This is a messy job, and almost always requires a dumpster on the premises. Then they apply a waterproof covering or membrane to the top of the roof deck. This is followed by a heavy-duty vapor barrier and some rigid insulation boards. The system is completed by covering the insulation with a topcoat of hot tar. Sometimes aggregate of some type (often small stones) is spread over the topcoat to protect the roofing from high winds and high temperatures.

Insulating from below the ceiling

If you live in an old house that has no insulation and you have a room below a flat roof or a cathedral ceiling, the prospect of tearing off the ceiling plaster or the roofing to get at the rafter cavities may be daunting. And it should be. Both jobs are difficult, expensive, and create a terrible mess. In some situations, it's better to pay high heating bills than to do what needs to be done to add some insulation.

There is another option: installing rigid insulation below the ceiling joists. To do this job, start by nailing or screwing 2 x 2 boards to the underside of the ceiling. Run these boards

perpendicular to the direction of the joists. Make sure the fasteners you use are long enough to extend through the 2 x 2s and plaster (or drywall), and into at least 2 inches of the joists.

Then, cut rigid insulation boards to fit between the 2 x 2s and glue them to the ceiling with construction adhesive. Once all the insulation is installed, cover the boards and the 2 x 2s with a polyethylene-sheet vapor barrier. Then screw or nail new drywall in place and finish the seams with tape and joint compound. Paint the ceiling with primer and then two coats of acrylic latex paint.

Fiberglass In new construction, or on major remodeling jobs, installing fiberglass batts or blankets between the studs is the most common and practical method for insulating walls. The thickness of the insulation you install depends on the width of the lumber used for the wall studs.

A typical wall, built with 2 x 4 lumber and finished on the inside with drywall and on the outside with wood siding, has an R-value of about 5 without any insulation in place. Installing 3½ inches of fiberglass raises the R-value to at least 16.

Loose fill With finished walls, the most common practice is to have a contractor drill holes through the exterior of the house and blow loose-fill insulation into the cavities between the studs. This usually delivers about R-12 rating. But for most homeowners, this is a job best left to professional insulation contractors. Equipment is available at rental centers if you want to blow in loose-fill insulation yourself.

Rigid foam If you are planning—or are willing—to re-side your house, adding rigid insulation over the sheathing before re-siding is a good idea. The insulation is nailed in place, the seams covered with duct tape, and the joints next to trim boards and other fixtures are filled with exterior-grade caulk. The new siding is installed over the insulation.

This system works well. It provides some insulating value and greatly reduces cold-air infiltration. But it is expensive and worth it only if you need new siding. Some vinyl siding products come with rigid-foam inserts that fit behind the siding panels. This raises the R-value of the wall even more.

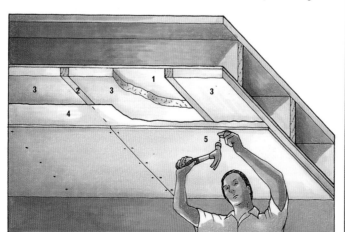

Insulating the ceiling
1 Existing drywall or plaster ceiling
2 Softwood 2 x 2s screwed to the joists
3 Insulation glued to existing ceiling
4 Polyethylene vapor barrier stapled to the 2 x 2s
5 Drywall nailed to the 2 x 2s

Although a great amount of heat escapes through the walls of a house, installing insulation in finished walls can be more expensive than the savings you get in reduced fuel bills. If you have no insulation in your walls, plan on a payback period of 5 to 10 years. (The shorter time applies to cold climates, the longer one to mild climates.) If the walls already contain some insulation, it could take as long as 25 years for energy savings to match the cost of adding more insulation.

Installing fiberglass blankets

Choose insulation wide enough to fit tightly between wall studs. To cut, unroll the insulation facing-side down, then use a framing square or straight board to compress the insulation and act as a cutting guide. Cut the insulation 2 inches longer than the bay, using a utility knife. Afterward, pull the facing away from the fiberglass at each end to create 1-inch stapling tabs.

Press the insulation into each bay, with the facing toward the room. With foil-faced material, staple the tabs to the inside faces of the studs so the insulation is recessed at least ¾ inch. With paper-faced material, staple the tabs flat along the outer edges of the studs, leaving no recess. Fit insulation behind obstructions, such as pipes and electrical boxes, so it lies against the exterior sheathing. Pack unfaced insulation into gaps between window and doorframes.

After installation is complete, staple a polyethylene vapor barrier across the entire wall, allowing the plastic to extend a few inches all around—to be covered later by finished ceiling, floor, and adjacent wallcovering. Carefully cut out around windows, doors, electrical boxes, and other openings before attaching interior wallcovering.

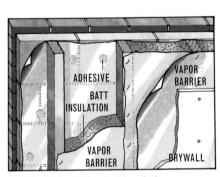

Details for installing batt insulation

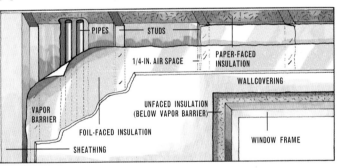

Details for installing batt insulation

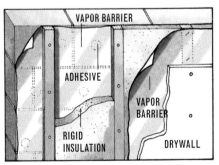

Details for installing rigid insulation

Safety

Fiberglass and mineral wool can severely irritate skin, lungs, eyes, and mucous membranes. When handling, always wear long sleeves and pants, gloves, goggles, and a respirator.

Insulating masonry walls

Above ground, masonry walls can be insulated with either blanket or rigid insulation. Below ground, because blanket insulation is susceptible to moisture damage, only rigid foam is recommended. (If you live in an extremely cold climate, insulating basement walls can cause foundation damage. Be sure to check with a local building inspector before proceeding.)

To apply blanket insulation, first cover the masonry surface with a polyethylene vapor barrier, attaching it with dabs of construction adhesive. Then, construct an ordinary stud wall against the masonry, nailing it to the floor and ceiling. Pack the bays with insulation, as described on this page. Cover the insulation with a second vapor barrier before finishing with drywall, paneling, or plaster.

To install rigid insulation, first attach a vapor barrier to the masonry, then nail vertical 1 x 2 furring strips to the wall, spaced 16 inches apart on center. Use masonry nails or cut nails for this job. You can also use concrete screws, which take longer to install and cost more than nails, but do a much better job of holding furring in place. Press insulation panels into the bays between strips. Make sure you have a snug fit. Then, cover the wall with a vapor barrier and the finished wallcovering, fastened to the furring strips.

Insulating floors

Air ducts and pipes

Even with carpet or other covering above, heat can readily escape through the ground floor into an unheated basement or crawlspace below.

Floors are best insulated from underneath by pressing fiberglass or mineral-wool insulation between the floor joists, much the same way as in insulating a stud-frame wall. Foil-faced insulation is the best choice, since it reflects escaping heat back in the direction it came from. Because joists are normally wider than wall studs, greater thicknesses of insulation may be used. Insulation may be pressed snugly against the subfloor (allow a ¾-inch gap if using foil-faced insulation), or fastened level with the bottom edges of the joists. Be sure the insulation extends over the foundation sills at

the ends of the joists. This is a primary heat-loss area.

Whether you use foil- or paper-faced insulation, the facing, which acts as a vapor barrier, must face the warm living space above. This makes fastening the insulation in place difficult, because the tabs on each side are no longer accessible. One solution is to staple wire mesh, such as chicken wire, across the joist edges as you install the insulation. Another solution—recommended especially if a basement ceiling will be installed—is to cut lengths of stiff wire, each slightly longer than the distances between joists, and press these wires, at 18- to 20-inch intervals, up into each bay to hold the insulation in place.

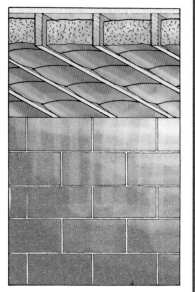

Insulating from below.
To secure insulation between floor joists, either staple wire mesh to the lower edges of the joists (right) or press lengths of heavy wire between the joists (far right).

Crawlspaces

It is seldom necessary to fully insulate crawlspaces, provided insulation is installed beneath the house floor above. A polyethylene vapor barrier should be spread over the crawlspace floor and extended at least partway up the walls to prevent moisture buildup. The space itself should be adequately vented to the outside. The vapor barrier may be left exposed if the space is unused.

If insulation is required, proceed as described earlier for insulating a masonry wall. Or, you can merely drape fiberglass batts down from the top of the foundation. Anchor the insulation with bricks along the top and with bricks or a length of 2 x 4 lumber at the bottom.

Hot-air ducts running through unheated basements or crawlspaces should be insulated to prevent heat loss, unless such loss is desirable to warm the space. Also, ducts carrying air from central air-conditioning systems should be insulated to retain cool air if they pass through areas that are not air-conditioned. Fiberglass and mineral-wool blanket insulation, with and without a reflective vapor barrier, are sold for this purpose at heating and air-conditioning supply stores. Choose reflective-barrier insulation for air-conditioning ducts. Ordinarily, no barrier is needed for hot-air ducts.

To install the insulation, cut it into sections where necessary, wrap it around the duct, then secure the seams with duct tape.

Exposed steam and hot-water pipes should also be insulated. For these, purchase foam insulation sleeves sold especially for the purpose at plumbing and hardware stores. The sleeves are slit along one side. To install, slip the sleeve over the pipe, then seal the seam with duct tape. Insulated, adhesive pipe-wrapping is also available. To attach this, merely remove the backing paper, then wrap the tape in a spiral, overlapping it slightly, around the pipe along its entire exposed length.

Blanket insulation for ducts

Foam insulation for pipes

Insulation tape for pipes

Double glazing

A double-glazed window consists of two sheets of glass separated by an air gap. The air gap provides an insulating layer that reduces heat loss and sound transmission. Condensation is also reduced, because the inner layer of glass remains warmer than the glass on the outside.

Both factory-sealed units and secondary glazing are used for domestic double glazing. Sealed units are unobtrusive, while secondary glazing is cheaper and helps to reduce the noise from outside. Both provide good thermal insulation.

What size air gap?

For heat insulation, a ¾-inch gap will give the optimum level of efficiency. If the gap is less than ½ inch, the air can conduct a proportion of the heat across the gap. If it's greater than ¾ inch, there is no appreciable gain in thermal insulation, and air currents can transmit heat to the outside layer of glass.

For noise insulation, an air gap of 4 to 8 inches is more effective. Triple glazing—a combination of sealed units with secondary glazing—may be the best solution.

The amount of heat lost from your house through windows is significant; a rule of thumb is about 10 to 12 percent. The installation of double glazing can cut this loss in half.

Another benefit is the elimination of drafts. Cold spots, experienced when sitting close to large windows, will be reduced too.

Installing double glazing with good window locks will also improve security against forced entry, partic-ularly when sealed units or tempered glass are used. However, make sure that some accessible part of appro-priate windows can be opened in order to provide an escape route in case of fire.

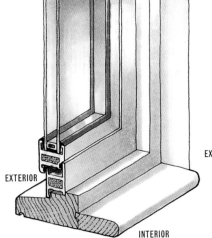

Factory-sealed unit
A complete frame system installed by a contractor.

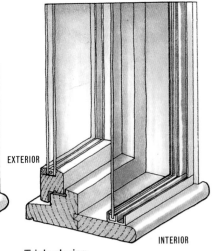

Secondary double glazing
Installed in addition to a single-glazed window.

Triple glazing
A combination of secondary and sealed units.

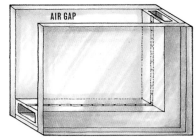

Double-glazed sealed unit

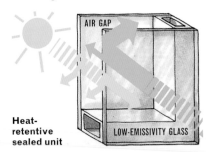

Heat-retentive sealed unit

Double-glazed sealed units

Double-glazed sealed units consist of two panes of glass that are separated by a spacer and hermetically sealed all around. The gap may contain dehydrated air, which eliminates condensation between the two panes of glass, or inert gases, which also improve thermal and acoustic insulation.

The thickness and type of glass used are determined by the size of the unit. Clear float glass or tempered glass is commonly employed. When obscured glazing is required to provide privacy, patterned glass is used. Heat-retentive sealed units, incorporating special low-emissivity glass, are offered by many window manufacturers.

Generally, factory-sealed units are installed by contractors or builders. But you can also buy sealed units that you can install yourself, particularly in the replacement-window marketplace. And, of course, you can have windows custom-made at some cabinetmaking shops. This option gives you just what you want, but for most people is prohibitively expensive.

Double-glazed sealed units with vinyl or aluminum frames are popular because they require almost no exterior maintenance. But these windows are not always appealing on older houses. A secondary system—similar to traditional storm windows—that leaves the original window intact is a better option for most restoration work.

Secondary double glazing

Glazing locations

Secondary double glazing consists of a separate pane of glass or sheet of plastic fitted over an ordinary single-glazed window. It is normally installed on the inside of existing windows, and is one of the more popular methods of double glazing. It's easy to install yourself and much cheaper than new, sealed units.

How the glazing is mounted

Secondary glazing can be fastened to the sash frame **(1, right)** or window frame **(2)**, or across the window reveal **(3)**. The method depends on the ease of installation, the type of glazing chosen, and the amount of ventilation needed.

Glazing mounted to the sash will reduce heat loss through the glass and provide accessible ventilation, but it won't stop drafts. Glazing attached to the window frame has the advantage of cutting down heat loss and eliminating drafts at the same time. Glazing installed across the reveal offers improved noise insulation too, since the air gap can be wider. Any system should be easy to remove, or preferably to open, to provide a change of air, especially if the room doesn't have any other form of ventilation.

A rigid plastic or glass pane can be mounted to the exterior of the window. Windows set in a deep reveal are generally the most suitable ones for external secondary glazing **(4)**.

● **Providing a fire escape.**
If you fit secondary glazing, make sure there is at least one window in every occupied room that can be opened easily.

Glazing with plastic film

Quite effective double glazing can be achieved using double-sided adhesive tape to stretch a thin flexible sheet of plastic across a window frame. The taped sheet can be removed at the end of the winter.

Clean the window frame **(1)** and cut the plastic roughly to size, allowing an overlap all around. Apply double-sided tape to the edges of the frame **(2)**, then peel off the backing paper.

Attach the plastic film to the top rail **(3)**, then pull it tightly onto the tape on the sides and bottom of the window frame **(4)**. Apply only light pressure until you have positioned the film, then rub it down onto all the tape.

Remove all creases and wrinkles in the film using a hair dryer set at high temperature **(5)**. Starting at an upper corner, move the dryer slowly across the film, holding it about ¼ inch from the surface. When the film is taut, cut off the excess plastic with a knife **(6)**.

Secondary double glazing, in one form or another, is particularly suitable for DIY installation. It's possible to fit a secondary system to almost any style or shape of window, from a traditional double-hung window to a modern casement.

1 Sash
Glazing attached to sash of window.

2 Frame
Glazing attached to structural frame.

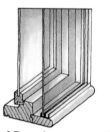

3 Reveal
Glazing mounted to reveal and interior windowsill.

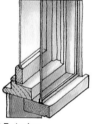

4 Exterior
Glazing attached to reveal and exterior windowsill.

1 Clean woodwork to remove dust and grease

2 Apply double-sided tape to window frame.

3 Stretch film across the top of frame

4 Pull film taut and press to sides and bottom

5 Use a hair dryer to shrink film

6 Trim waste with a sharp knife

Plastic double glazing

Removable systems

A simple method of interior secondary glazing uses clear plastic film or sheeting. These lightweight materials are held in place by self-adhesive strips or rigid molded strips, which form a seal. Most strip fastenings use magnetism, which allows the secondary glazing to be removed for cleaning or ventilation. The strips and tapes usually have a flexible foam backing, which takes up slight irregularities in the woodwork. This type of glazing can be left in place throughout the winter and removed for storage during the summer months.

Installing a removable system Clean the windows and the surfaces of the window frame. Cut the plastic sheet to size, then hold it against the window frame and draw around it **(1)**. Lay the sheet on a flat table. Peel back the protective paper from one end of the self-adhesive strip and stick it to the plastic sheet, flush with one edge. Cut the strip to length and repeat on the other edges. Cut the mating parts of the strips and stick them onto the window frame, following the guide-lines marked earlier. Press the glazing into place **(2)**.

When using rigid molded sections, cut the sections to length with mitered corners. To attach an extruded molding **(3)**, stick the base section to the frame, then insert the outer section to hold the glazing in place.

1 Mark around glazing

2 Position glazed unit

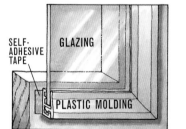

SELF-ADHESIVE TAPE

GLAZING

PLASTIC MOLDING

3 Rigid plastic moldings support glazing

Plastic materials for double glazing

Plastic materials can be used in place of glass to provide lightweight double glazing. They are available as clear, thin flexible film and as clear textured or colored rigid sheets.

Unlike glass windows, plastic glazing has a high impact resistance and does not splinter when broken. Depending on its thickness, plastic can be cut with scissors, drilled, sawn, planed, or filed.

The clarity of the newer types of plastics is as good as that of glass. Although they have the disadvantage of being easily scratched, slight abrasions can be rubbed out with metal polish. Plastics are also liable to degrade with age, and are prone to static. It's best to wash plastic sheeting with a liquid soap solution.

Film and semirigid plastics are sold by the square foot or in rolls. Rigid sheets are available in a range of standard sizes, or can be cut to order.

Rigid plastic sheets are generally supplied with a protective covering of paper or thin plastic on both faces. In order to avoid scratching the surface of the sheets, don't peel off the covering until after cutting and shaping.

Polyester film Polyester film is a form of plastic often used for inexpensive secondary double glazing. It can be trimmed with scissors or a knife and attached with self-adhesive tape or strip fasteners. The fact that polyester is tough, virtually tearproof, and very clear makes it an ideal plastic for glazing windows.

Polystyrene Polystyrene is an inexpensive plastic that is available in both clear and textured sheet form. Clear polystyrene doesn't have the clarity of glass, and degrades in strong sunlight, so it shouldn't be used for south-facing windows or for situations where a distortion-free view is desirable. Depending on the climate, the life of polystyrene is estimated to be between three and five years. Its working life can be extended if the glazing is removed for storage in the summer.

Acrylic Acrylic is a good-quality rigid plastic. It is up to ten times as strong as glass, without any loss in clarity. Although it costs approximately twice as much as polystyrene, the working life of acrylic is estimated to be at least 15 years. It is manufactured in a useful range of translucent and opaque colors.

Polycarbonate A lightweight, vandalproof glazing with a high level of clarity, this plastic is most commonly available in $\frac{1}{16}$-, $\frac{1}{8}$-, and $\frac{5}{32}$-inch-thick sheets. It costs about twice what acrylic costs. Polycarbonate sheeting has a hollow ribbed section that gives it exceptional rigidity, while at the same time keeping both heat loss and weight to a minimum.

PVC glazing PVC is available as a flexible film or rigid sheet that is ultraviolet stabilized and therefore unaffected by sunlight. PVC film provides inexpensive glazing where a high degree of clarity is not essential, such as in the basement or attic.

Storm window systems

Secondary glazing applied to the exterior of windows usually takes the form of storm sashes, either one-piece, single-pane windows that are installed in the fall and taken down in spring, or permanently mounted, sliding-sash panes that remain in place all year. Single-pane storm windows can be homemade, often at considerable savings over purchased windows. However, installing sliding windows is best left to professional storm-window installers.

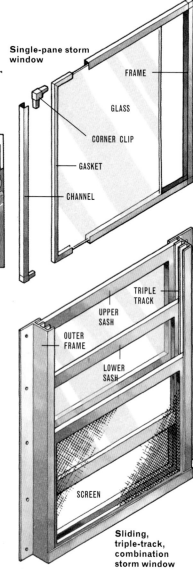

Single-pane storm window

FRAME

GLASS

CORNER CLIP

GASKET

CHANNEL

Storm window mounting details

● **Sliding storm windows**
When having storms installed, be sure caulk is applied to the existing frame before the storm frame is mounted. And, always make sure the windows operate smoothly before accepting the job.

TRIPLE TRACK

UPPER SASH

OUTER FRAME

LOWER SASH

SCREEN

Sliding, triple-track, combination storm window

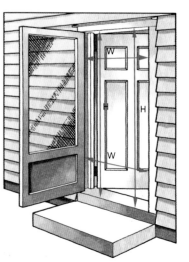

Combination storm/screen door
To fit, measure height (H) and width (W) of door opening in at least two places.

How to make a single-pane storm window

Measure the length and width of the window opening by holding the tape against the outside edges of the blind stop against which the storm window will sit. Single-pane storm-window kits are often available at hardware stores and home centers. If you can't find a kit in the size you need, purchase lengths of aluminum storm-window channel (prefitted with a U-shaped rubber glazing gasket), and friction-fit corner clips (usually sold with the channel) to make the frame. Don't attempt to make windows taller than 5 feet, because such large areas of glass are hard to handle.

Remove the gasket, then cut four pieces of channel so that when assembled, the outside dimension of the frame measures ⅛ inch less in both height and width than the window opening. Assemble three sides of the frame using the corner clips to hold the pieces together. Drive the clips into the channel ends using a small ball-peen hammer.

Purchase double-strength glass for the pane, cut so it will fit between the channels of the frame with the gasket installed. Fit the gasket around the edge of the pane, mitering the gasket sides at each corner with a utility knife (discard the triangular scraps of waste gasket), then slide the pane into the frame and install the final length of channel.

Attach two-piece, storm-window hanging brackets from the top edge of the storm window, then mount the window to the outside of the opening. The storm window should sit firmly. However, you may wish to fasten it at the bottom and apply removable weather stripping around the inside.

Sliding storm windows

Sliding storm windows, usually called combination windows (because they incorporate a screen for use during summer), are available from home and building supply centers. Most often, they are designed to fit the outside of double-hung window frames, and can be operated merely by raising the interior window to gain access to the latches controlling each sash. In triple-track units, the upper storm-window sash is mounted—sometimes permanently—on the outermost track of the storm-window frame. The lower sash slides up and down in the middle track, and a screen slides up and down in the innermost track. In double-track units, the lower sash and screen are interchangeable, to be switched according to season.

It's important that sliding storm windows are well made and tight fitting. When purchasing, look for quality corner construction, gasketing on both sides of the glass, and deep tracks in the channel. Metal latches are more durable than plastic ones. At the bottom of each frame should be small (¼-inch-diameter) holes to prevent condensation.

Combination storm and screen doors

Combination storm doors are usually made of aluminum. However, wood doors offer greater energy savings. Both are usually sold mounted in a frame, ready for installation. To measure the door opening, measure both the height and the width in at least two places. Use the smallest measurement in each case. For the height, measure between the doorsill and the inside face of the head jamb. For the width, measure between the two door rabbets in the side jambs. On most entry doors, there will be a flat surface already milled into the doorjambs to accept a screen, storm, or combination door.

Ventilation

Ventilation is essential for a fresh, comfortable atmosphere, but it has a more important function with regard to the structure of our homes. Ventilation wasn't a problem when houses were heated with open fires, drawing fresh air through all the natural openings in the structure. With the introduction of central heating, insulation, and draftproofing, well-designed ventilation is vital. Without a constant change of air, centrally heated rooms quickly become stuffy. Before long, the moisture content of the air becomes so high that water easily condenses, often with serious consequences.

There are various ways to provide ventilation. Some are simple; others are much more sophisticated.

Initial consideration

Whenever you undertake an improve-ment that involves insulation in one form or another, take into account how it is likely to affect the existing ventilation. It may change conditions sufficiently to create trouble in areas outside the habitable rooms, where the symptoms can't be seen, such as under floorboards or in the attic. If there is a chance that damp conditions might result from a project, provide additional ventilation.

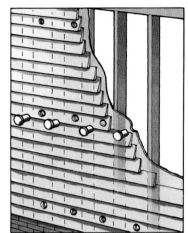

Ventilator plugs for drying out damp wall cavities

Ventilating wall cavities

Faulty vapor protection can lead to moisture accumulating within walls. The problem is common in renovated houses where insulation has been added to older buildings. Suspect the need for ventilation especially if you notice blistering paint on the exterior of the house.

To ventilate wall cavities, install vent plugs, small cylindrical louvers available in several diameters from hardware and building supply stores. Drill holes from the exterior of the house into each cavity where moisture is suspected, at the bottom, top, and at 4-foot intervals in between, and insert the plugs.

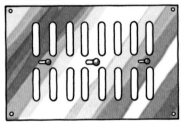

Operable ventilator

Ventilating a fireplace

An open fire needs oxygen to burn brightly. If the supply is reduced by thorough draftproofing or double glazing, the fire smolders and the slightest downdraft blows smoke into the room. There may be other reasons why a fire burns poorly—a blocked chimney for example. But if the fire picks up within minutes of partially opening the door to the room, you can be sure that inadequate ventilation is the problem.

One efficient and attractive solution is to cut holes in the floorboards on each side of the fireplace and cover them with a ventilator. Cheap plastic grilles work just as well, but you may prefer brass or aluminum for a living room. Choose an operable ventilator, which you can open and close to seal off unwelcome drafts when the fire is not in use. If the room has carpeting, cut a hole in it and screw the ventilator into the floor.

Another solution is to install a sealed fireplace-door unit, which comes with inlet pipes and a small blower. Cut holes in the exterior wall at each side of the fireplace, insert the pipes, and attach vents on the outside.

Ventilating an unused fireplace An unused fireplace that has been blocked by bricks, blocks, or drywall should be ventilated to allow air to flow up the chimney and dry out any moisture. Some people believe a vent from a warm interior aggravates the problem by introducing moist air to condense on the cold surface of the brick flue. However, as long as the chimney is uncapped, the updraft should draw moisture-laden air to the outside. A brick vent installed in the flue from outside is a safer solution, but it is more difficult to accomplish and, of course, impossible if the chimney is located within the house. Furthermore, the vent will have to be blocked if you want to reopen the fireplace later.

To ventilate from inside the room, leave out a single brick or block, or cut a hole in the drywall. Then, cover the hole with a ventilator that's at least ½ inch wider and higher than the hole.

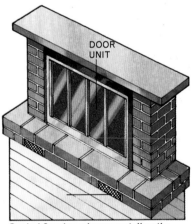

Sealed fireplace doors vent directly outdoors

Face-mounted ventilator for a fireplace

Ventilating below floors

Perforated openings known as air bricks are built into the external walls of a brick house to ventilate the space below the wood floors. If they become clogged with earth or leaves, there's a strong possibility of dry rot developing in the wood framing members. So, if you have a brick house, check the condition of air bricks regularly.

Checking out the air bricks

Ideally, there ought to be an air brick every 6 feet along an external wall, but in many brick buildings the air bricks are spaced farther apart without any harm being done. Sufficient airflow is more important than the actual number of openings in the wall.

In some older brick homes, the floor joists that span a wide room are supported at intervals by low sleeper walls made of brick. Sometimes these are perforated to facilitate an even airflow throughout the space. In other cases, there are merely gaps left by the builder between sections of solid wall. This method of constructing sleeper walls can lead to pockets of still air in corners that drafts never reach.

Even when all the air bricks are clear, dry rot can break out in areas that don't receive an adequate change of air. If you suspect there are dead areas under your floor (particularly if there are signs of damp or mold growth), install an additional air brick in a wall nearby.

Old ceramic air bricks sometimes get broken, and are often ignored because there is no detrimental effect on the ventilation. However, even a small hole can provide access for vermin. Don't be tempted to block the opening, even temporarily. Instead, replace the broken air brick with a similar one of the same size. You can choose from single or double air bricks, made from ceramic or plastic.

Installing or replacing an air brick

Use a masonry drill to remove the mortar surrounding the brick you are removing, and a cold chisel to chop out the brick itself. Spread mortar on the base of the hole and along the top and both sides of the new air brick. Push it into the opening, keeping it flush with the face of the exterior brick. Repoint the mortar to match the profile used on the surrounding wall.

To build an air brick into a cavity wall, bridge the gap with a plastic telescoping unit, which is mortared into the hole from both sides. The telescoping function allows the unit to fit a range of different wall thicknesses. If need be, a ventilator grille can be screwed to the inner end of the unit.

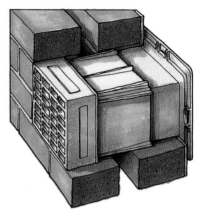

Air brick with telescoping sleeve
Bridge a cavity wall with this type of unit.

Cavity tray
A cavity tray sheds any moisture that penetrates the cavity wall above the unit. It is necessary only when the air brick is fitted above the damp-proof course on the house wall.

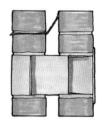

Single ceramic brick

Double plastic air brick

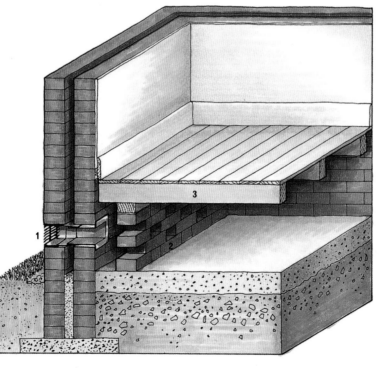

Ventilating the space below a wood floor.
The illustration (left) shows a cross section through a typical, brick cavity-wall structure, with a wood floor suspended over a concrete slab. A house with solid-brick walls is ventilated in a similar way.
1 Air brick fitted with sleeve.
2 Sleeper wall built with staggered bricks to allow air to circulate.
3 Floorboards and joists are susceptible to dry rot caused by poor ventilation.

Roof venting patterns

Ventilating the roof space

Because warm air rises, air entering through the eaves is most effectively vented at or near the ridge. Below are some common venting arrangements.

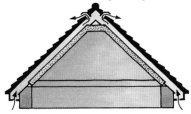

An attic space If insulating between rafters, provide a minimum 2-inch airway between the insulation and the roof sheathing. Install soffit vents and roof vents.

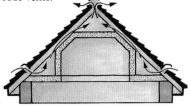

An attic room Install a ridge vent and roof vents (as close to the eaves as possible) to draw air around an insulated attic room.

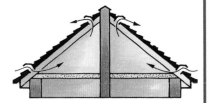

A fire wall A solid wall built across an attic space prevents eaves-to-eaves ventilation. Install roof vents near the eaves and near the ridge on both sides of the roof.

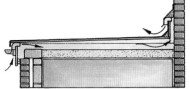

A flat roof An insulated flat roof can be ventilated by installing continuous soffit vents along the eaves and above the fascia board where the roof meets the house.

When attic insulation first became popular as an energy-saving measure, many people were told to tuck insulation right into the eaves to keep out drafts. What this advice failed to recognize was that a free flow of air is necessary in the roof space to prevent moisture-laden air from condensing on the structure.

Inadequate ventilation can lead to serious deterioration. Wet rot can develop in the roof framing, and water can drip onto the insulation, eventually rendering it ineffective. If water builds up into pools, the ceiling below becomes stained and there is a risk of short-circuiting the electrical wiring throughout the attic. For these reasons, efficient ventilation of the roof space is essential.

Ventilating the eaves

Building codes specify ventilation requirements, so check with your local building department before installing vents yourself. One common rule of thumb is 1 square foot of ventilation opening for every 300 square feet of roof.

The best configuration of ventilators for your house depends on how much air needs to circulate and the way your roof has been framed. Most standard gable roofs include either vent plugs or continuous vent strips in the soffit under the eaves. Both types of vents have screened backs to keep insects out. These soffit vents are usually combined with louvered vents at the top of both gable ends. In houses that don't have gable roofs, gable vents are replaced by roof vents cut into the back side of the roof near the ridge.

Soffit vent

Both systems work well, until any of the components are blocked and the air can't get through. This can happen, particularly when extra insulation is added to the attic and is pushed down over the top of soffit vents. Always allow uninterrupted air flow over any new insulation.

Installing eaves vents

In houses where soffit vents are not installed, adding the plug-type vents is easier than the continuous-strip vents. Just drill holes in the soffit between all the rafters and push the vents into these holes. If necessary, install baffles between the rafters to keep the insulation from blocking the airflow.

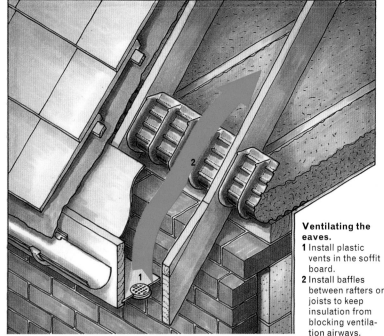

Ventilating the eaves.
1 Install plastic vents in the soffit board.
2 Install baffles between rafters or joists to keep insulation from blocking ventilation airways.

As mentioned earlier, the proper amount of roof ventilation is an issue controlled by local building codes. So make sure to ask for these guidelines from the building inspector. A good rule of thumb is 1 square foot of open ventilation for every 300 square feet of attic area. For a house with 1200 square feet of attic, the total vent area would have to be at least 4 square feet. This rule assumes a vapor barrier is in place below the attic floor.

If no vapor barrier is in place to restrict some of the moisture flow into the attic, then the ventilation requirements increase. The rule of thumb for this situation is 1 square foot of open ventilation for every 150 square feet of attic area. Using the 1200-square-foot attic example from above, the house without a vapor barrier would require 8 square feet of venting.

Unless the local code has other recommendations, your goal is to split the ventilation square footage as evenly as possible between the eaves and the ridge. So on a typical gable roof with a vapor barrier in place, you'd want about 1 square foot of ventilation incorporated into each of the eaves, and 1 square foot on both sides of the ridge.

Thirty years ago, the standard approach would have been to install a rectangular vent every 6 to 10 feet along the soffits and a triangular gable vent on both ends of the house, or a couple of roof vents near the ridge on the back side of the house.

But now that we know how important proper ventilation is to the long-term health of a house, the tendency has been to increase this ventilation substantially. These days, it's common to have a 1½-inch continuous vent built into each soffit and a continuous ridge vent installed along the full length of the roof ridge. This arrangement provides more, and better, airflow because there are no pockets of dead air in the attic that aren't moved out. Each rafter or truss bay is continually bathed in fresh air from the bottom to the top.

Installing a ridge vent

A continuous ventilating strip running the length of the roof provides very effective outflow ventilation. Ridge venting may be installed on any pitched roof, during new construction or reroofing, or as a task by itself.

If a ridge vent is to be included in the new construction of a roof, the roof decking is laid to leave a gap on either side of the ridge board, creating an open slot along the roof peak approximately 2 inches wide.

Determine the actual width from the size of the ridge vent. The gap allows exiting air to pass through. If felt roofing paper is laid, trim it even with the top edge of the sheathing. Fasten the ridge vent over the gap, nailing it into the decking and rafters on both sides. Lay the final course of shingles on each side of the roof so that they cover the base of the vent.

Installing roof ventilators

Installing ventilators on the sloping portions of a roof requires careful cutting and sealing to prevent leaks. You may want to hire a professional roofer to do the job.

First, determine the location of the vent. It must lie between rafters. Use the vent itself or a template made of cardboard (sometimes supplied with the vent) to mark the area of the roof to be cut out. It should be smaller than the overall dimensions of the vent base so that the vent can be pushed beneath adjacent shingles. Cut out the area by first

To install a ridge vent to a finished roof, you will have to cut a gap along the roof peak to create a passage for exiting air. Use a chalkline to mark the cutting line on each side of the peak, then cut through the shingles and felt paper first, using a utility knife, to expose the sheathing. Set the blade of a circular saw slightly deeper than the thickness of the sheathing, then cut along each chalked line to open the roof. Be careful to avoid nails.

Caulk the underside of the ridge-vent sides, then fasten it over the slot using roofing nails long enough to penetrate at least 1½ inches into the rafters.

removing the roofing (use a utility knife to cut through asphalt shingles), then sawing through the wood sheathing using a sabre saw. Apply plastic roof cement to the underside of the vent. Then slide it into place and fasten it with galvanized roofing nails. As you slide the vent in, you'll have to hold up the neighboring shingles so the top of the vent rests flat against the sheathing. Cover the nailheads with cement, and smooth down the shingles around the vent so they lay flat. Glue them in place with roof cement.

Extractor fans

Since kitchens and bathrooms are particularly prone to condensation, it's important to have some means of expelling moisture-laden air and unpleasant odors. An electrical extractor fan can freshen a room quickly without creating drafts.

Locating the fan

The best place to site a fan is either in a window or on an outside wall, but its exact location depends on where the room door is. Stale air extracted from the room must be replaced by fresh air, which normally happens through the door leading to other areas of the house. But if the fan is too close to the source of replacement air, it will draw air directly from the doorway and have little effect on the rest of the room. The ideal position for the fan is directly opposite the source of replacement air, as high as possible, to extract the hot air **(1)**. In a kitchen, try to locate the fan above or adjacent to the range, so that cooking smells and steam will not be drawn across the room before being expelled **(2)**.

If the room contains a fuel-burning appliance with a flue, you must make sure that there is enough replacement air to prevent fumes from the appliance from being drawn down the flue when the extractor fan is switched on.

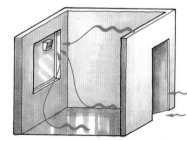

1 Install fan opposite replacement-air source

2 In a kitchen, place extractor near range

Types of extractor fans

Many fans have an integral switch. If not, a switched connection unit can be wired into the circuit when you install the fan. Some types incorporate a built-in controller to regulate the speed of extraction, and a timer that switches off the fan after a certain interval. Some fans will switch on automatically when the humidity in the room reaches a predetermined level. Axial fans can be installed in a window, and with the addition of a duct, some models will extract air through a wall. To overcome the pressure resistance in a long run of ducting, a centrifugal fan may be required. To prevent backdrafts, choose a fan with external shutters that close when the fan is not in use.

Window-mounted axial fan
1 Inner casing
2 Motor assembly
3 Interior clamping plate
4 Glass
5 Grille-clamping plate
6 Exterior grille

Wall-mounted axial fan
1 Motor assembly
2 Interior backplate
3 Duct
4 Exterior grille

● **Low-voltage fans**
A low-voltage fan, which comes with its own transformer, can be mounted directly above a shower.

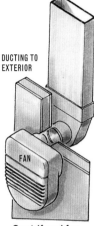

DUCTING TO EXTERIOR

FAN

Centrifugal fan

Choosing the size of a fan

The size of a fan, or to be accurate, its capacity, should be determined by the type of room in which it is installed and the volume of air it has to move.

A fan installed in a kitchen must be capable of changing the air completely 10 to 15 times per hour. A bathroom requires 6 to 8 air changes per hour, or 15 to 20 changes if a shower is installed. A living room normally requires about 4 to 6 changes per hour, but it's best to install a fan with a slightly larger capacity if the room will be smoky.

In order to determine the minimum capacity required, calculate the volume of the room (length x width x height) and then multiply the volume by the recommended number of air changes per hour (see example below).

CALCULATING THE CAPACITY OF A FAN FOR A KITCHEN			
Size of kitchen			
Length	**Width**	**Height**	**Volume**
11 ft.	10 ft.	8 ft.	880 cu. ft.

Air changes		**Volume**	**Fan capacity**
15 per hour	x	880 cu. ft.	13,200 cu. ft.

Installing a wall-mounted fan

Window-mounted fans

● Before you begin
Make sure there are no plumbing pipes, electrical wiring, or other obstructions buried in the wall.

Metal detector
Detect buried pipes or wiring with an electronic sensor placed against the wall.

1 Seal plate spigot

2 Insert duct in hole

3 Screw-fix grille

Cutting the hole Wall-mounted fans are supplied with a length of plastic ducting for inserting in a hole cut through the wall. Mark the center of the hole and draw its diameter on the inside of the wall. Use a long masonry drill to bore a hole through the wall.

If you have masonry walls on the outside of your house, use this fit hole as a reference point for the center of the vent duct. Hold the duct up to the wall and trace around it. Then, bore a series of holes through the masonry with a masonry bit. The more holes you drill, the easier it will be to remove the bricks, stones, or stucco. Use a cold chisel and a hammer to cut the masonry between the holes. Work carefully to create a hole as close to the duct size as possible. The exterior grille may not be able to cover a sloppy hole. Once the masonry is removed, cut away the wood sheathing with a reciprocating saw or a keyhole saw. Cut out the drywall or plaster on the inside of the house according to the fan maker's directions.

Installing the fan Separate the components of the fan, then attach a self-adhesive sealing strip to the backplate to receive the duct **(1)**.

Insert the duct in the hole so that the backplate fits against the wall **(2)**. Mark the length of the duct on the outside, remembering to allow for sliding the duct onto the outer grille. Cut the duct to length with a hacksaw. Reposition the backplate and duct in order to mark the installation holes on the wall. Drill the holes into the wall and install toggle bolts or wall anchors. Then, feed the electrical supply cable into the backplate before screwing the plate to the wall. Apply the sealing strip to the exterior grille and push it onto the duct. Mark and drill the mounting holes for the exterior grille, then screw it in place **(3)**. If the grille doesn't fit flush with the wall, seal the gap with caulk. Wire the fan according to the manufacturer's instructions, then attach the motor assembly to the mounting plate.

An extractor fan can be installed only in a fixed window. If you want to fit one in a sliding sash window, you will need to secure the top sash, in which the fan is installed, then fit a sash stop on each side of the window in order to prevent the lower sash from damaging the casing of the fan.

Cutting the glass Every window-mounted fan requires a round hole to be cut in the glass. The size is specified by the manufacturer. It is possible to cut a hole in an existing window, but stresses in the glass will sometimes cause it to crack. All things considered, it is generally better to install a new pane of glass that has been cut exactly to fit the requirements of the fan you bought.

Cutting a hole in glass is not easy for most people, so it's usually a better idea to have it cut by a local glass shop. You will need to provide exact dimensions, including the size and position of the hole. Order glass that matches the existing pane.

Installing the fan The exact assembly may vary, but the following sequence is a typical example of how a fan is installed in a window:

Take out the existing window pane

and clean up the frame, removing retaining points and traces of old putty. Then install the new pane with the precut hole.

To get a good seal, brush all the dust away from the window-frame rabbet and coat the rabbet with mineral spirits. Roll a golf-ball-size piece of glazing compound into a ¼-inch-thick rope and press it into the rabbet. Continue until you've worked your way around the entire window. Then, smooth the compound and remove the excess with a putty knife. Install the pane and glazier's points to keep it in place, then fill the rabbet with compound.

From outside, install the exterior grille by locating its circular flange in the hole **(1)**. Attach the plate on the inside to clamp the grille to the glass **(2)**. Tighten the installation screws carefully in rotation to achieve a good seal and an even clamping force on the glass. Screw the motor assembly to the clamping plate **(3)**. Wire the fan in accordance with the manufacturer's instructions. Then, install the inner housing over the motor assembly **(4)**.

Finally, switch on the fan to check that the mechanism runs smoothly and that the backdraft shutter opens and closes automatically when the unit is switched on and off.

1 Place grille in hole from outside

2 Screw inner and outer plates together

3 Screw motor assembly to plate

Warning
Never attempt to make electrical connections before you have switched off the power at the service panel.

4 Attach housing to cover assembly

Recirculation or extraction?

Some range hoods filter out odors and grease and then return the air to the room. Others direct stale air outside through a duct in the wall. The extraction design is generally considered the better option, though sometimes installing the duct can be so difficult and expensive that using the recirculating method makes more sense.

In order to install an extracting hood, it is necessary to cut a hole through the wall and install ducting. Although hoods that recycle the air are much simpler to install, they do not remove moisture from the room and do not filter out all of the grease and cooking odors. To keep any range hood working at peak efficiency, change or clean the filters regularly.

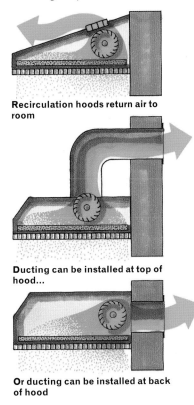

Recirculation hoods return air to room

Ducting can be installed at top of hood...

Or ducting can be installed at back of hood

Installing a range hood

Window-mounted and wall-mounted fans are primarily intended for overall room-air extraction. But the most effective way to rid your kitchen of water vapor and cooking smells is to mount a ventilator hood directly over your range or cooktop.

Where to mount the range hood

Unless the manufacturer's recommendations indicate otherwise, a range hood is typically positioned between 2 and 3 feet above a range or cooktop.

Depending on the model, a range hood may be either cantilevered from the wall or screwed between or beneath kitchen wall cabinets. Some cabinet manufacturers produce special range-hood housing units that match the style of their cabinets. If you're installing all new cabinets, you should consider ordering one of these.

Most range hoods have either two or three speed settings and built-in light fixtures to illuminate the cooking surface below.

Installing ducting

When a range hood is mounted on an external wall, air is pulled through the back of the unit into a straight duct passing through the wall.

But, if the range is situated against an interior wall, you'll need to connect the hood to the outside with ductwork. The straight and curved components of the standard duct simply plug into one another to form a continuous shaft running between the hood and the outside wall.

Placement of this duct is often a complicated job. You have to determine where there is space available. Sometimes the duct can run over the top of wall cabinets until it reaches an outside wall. This is the easiest solution, and requires only the addition of a valance or soffit on top of the cabinets to hide the duct from view. If this option isn't available to you, it makes sense to hire a contractor to install the duct elsewhere.

To install the duct, begin by attaching the female end of the first component to the top or back of the hood. Then continue piecing together sections of straight duct with elbows until you reach the outside wall. Cut a hole through the wall and install straight duct to the exterior grille.

Installing the hood

Range hoods are hung from brackets that are sold with them. These brackets are screwed either between wall cabinets or directly to the wall. Cut a hole through the wall (or the cabinets above) for the duct, and run new electrical cable to the hood for driving the fan.

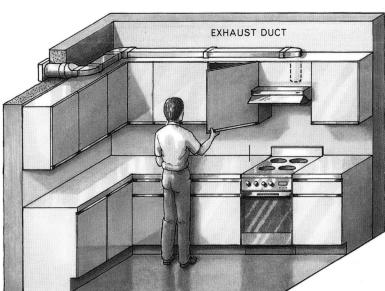

EXHAUST DUCT

Installing exhaust ducts. When a range is located against an interior wall, run the duct from the hood along the top of the wall cupboards.

Heat-recovery ventilation

It has been estimated that more than half the energy produced by burning fossil fuels is used to keep our homes warm. Although the installation of efficient insulation significantly reduces heat loss, a great deal of heat is still wasted as a result of ventilation.

Heat-recovery ventilators are designed to balance the requirements of conserving energy and the need for a constant supply of clean fresh air by capturing some of the heat from the air that's leaving the house and transferring it to the clean air coming in.

How a heat-recovery ventilator works

Heat-recovery ventilation unit
The diagram shows the layout of a typical wall-mounted heat-recovery ventilator.
1 Stale air from room
2 Stale air exhaust
3 Fresh air supply
4 Warmed fresh air
5 Heat exchanger
6 Induction fan
7 Exhaust fan

Heat-recovery ventilation can range in scale from compact units for continuous low-volume ventilation of individual rooms to whole-house ducted systems.

The simple ventilator shown here contains two low-noise electric fans. Stale air from the interior is extracted by one fan through a highly efficient heat exchanger. This absorbs up to 70 percent of the heat that would otherwise be wasted and transfers it to a flow of fresh air drawn into the room by the second fan. Because the two airflows are not allowed to mingle, odors and water vapor are not transferred along with the heat.

Self-contained heat-recovery ventilators can be installed in exterior walls or windows. The extraction unit of larger ducted systems is usually mounted in the basement, or sometimes in the attic.

Installing a heat-recovery ventilator

With the aid of a level, use the manufacturer's template to mark the position of the ventilator on the wall, including the centers of both ducts **(1)**. Locate the unit high on the the wall, but with at least a 2-inch clearance above and to the sides.

The ducting is likely to be narrower than that used for standard exhaust fans, so it may be possible to use a holesaw **(2)**. Drill a pilot hole through both the interior wallcovering and the exterior sheathing and siding first. After cutting the hole in the interior wall, cut the hole in the exterior wall slightly lower so that the ducting will slope to drain condensation to the outside. If the ducting is too large to

use a holesaw, use a keyhole or saber saw instead, and trim the holes using a rasp. Use a hacksaw to cut the ducting to a length that equals the depth of the wall plus ⅜ inch. Use aluminum flashing tape to hold both ducts to the back of the wall-mounting plate. Insert the ducting into the wall holes **(3)**, push the panel against the wall, and mount it with screws.

Outside, plug the gaps around the ducting with fiberglass insulation **(4)** and screw the covers over the ends of the ducts. Seal around the edges with caulk **(5)**. Fit the main unit to the mounting plate on the inside wall **(6)** and wire it to a nearby outlet box.

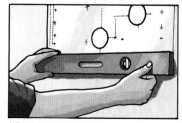
1 Position template to mark ducts and fasteners

2 Bore holes for ducting with holesaw

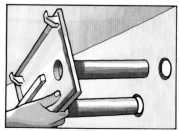
3 Pass ducts through wall

4 Plug gaps around ducts with insulation

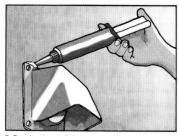
5 Seal edge of duct covers with caulk

6 Install ventilator unit on mounting plate

Mounting a flush ventilator

Most flush-mounted ventilators require a wooden frame to line a hole cut through the wall. Make it to the dimensions supplied by the man-ufacturer of the ventilator. Construct the frame with glued and screwed butt joints. Decide on the approximate position of the unit, then locate the wall studs to align one with the side of the unit. Mark the rectangle for the wooden lining onto the wall, then drill through the drywall or plaster at the corners of the outline. Cut out the rectangle with a keyhole saw or saber saw and remove the wall insulation. Working from outside, cut away the siding and sheathing along the same lines. Saw off any studs obstructing the hole flush with its edges. (Do not remove studs from a bearing wall without consulting a building inspector.)

Insert the lining. The ventilator must be angled downward a few degrees toward the outside to drain away condensation. If this angle is built into the ventilator unit, the wood-frame lining can be set flush with the wall. Otherwise, tilt the frame a fraction by shimming it underneath before nailing. Compare diagonal measurements to make sure the lining is square in the hole.

Slide the ventilator unit into the liner, screw it in place, and install the front panel. Outside, seal the joints between the sheathing, the lining, and the ventilator unit with caulk.

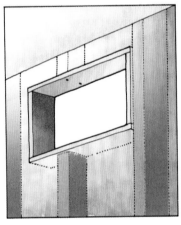

Mounting a flush ventilator
Install a wood-frame liner in the wall close to the ceiling where it will be in the best position to extract hot rising air. Attach the ventilator to the liner with screws.

Installing through a masonry wall

Decide on the approximate position of the unit, then mark its position on the wall by scribing around it with a pencil or awl. Use a masonry drill to bore a hole through the wall at each corner. Then cut through the drywall with a utility knife or through plaster with a cold chisel. Continue to drill holes around the perimeter of the hole and chop out the masonry with a cold chisel. After cutting halfway into the wall, drill a hole that goes the rest of the way through, using a long masonry bit. Use this hole as a reference point for drawing the cutout on the outside of the wall. Finish cutting the hole from the outside.

Mounting a ventilator liner   Clean up the rectangular hole you cut through the masonry. Then construct a wood liner using butt joints at the corners. Insert the liner, tilting it slightly toward the outside if necessary.

Mounting liner
1 Cut rectangular hole through masonry with cold chisel.
2 Build wood liner to fit size of ventilator and install in hole.
3 Slide ventilator into liner and attach.

To combat condensation, you can either remove the moisture-laden air by ventilation, or warm it so that it is able to carry more water vapor before it becomes saturated. A third possibility is to extract the water itself from the air using a dehumidifier.

A dehumidifier works by drawing air from the room into the unit and passing it over a set of cold coils, so that the water vapor condenses on them and drips into a reservoir. The cold (but now dry) air is then drawn by a fan over heated coils before being returned to the room as additional heat.

The process is based on the simple refrigeration principle that gas under pressure heats up—and when the pressure drops, the temperature of the gas drops too. In a dehumidifier, a compressor delivers pressurized gas to the hot coils, in turn leading to the larger cold coils, which allow the gas to expand. The cooled gas then returns to the compressor for recycling.

A dehumidifier for domestic use is usually built into a floor-standing cabinet. It contains a humidistat that automatically switches on the unit when the moisture content of the air reaches a predetermined level. When the reservoir is full, the unit shuts down in order to prevent over-flowing, and an indicator lights up to remind you to empty the water in the container. When a dehumidifier is installed in a damp room, it should extract the excess moisture from the furnishings and fabric within a week or two. After that, it will monitor the moisture content of the air to maintain a stabilized atmosphere.

A portable version can be wheeled from room to room, where it is plugged into a standard wall outlet.

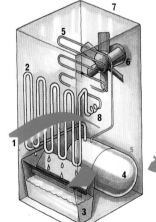

Working components of a dehumidifier
The diagram illustrates the layout of a typical domestic dehumidifier.
1 Incoming damp air
2 Cold coils
3 Water reservoir
4 Compressor
5 Hot coils
6 Fan
7 Dry warm air
8 Capillary tube where gas expands

Air conditioners

Choosing the capacity

Central air-conditioning systems should be checked once a year in early spring by a professional service technician. During the air-conditioning season, check and replace the filters once a month, or more frequently in dusty areas.

Even small window- or wall-mounted air conditioners are usually factory-sealed and lubricated. However, it is important to keep the indoor and outdoor grilles dust-free to maintain high cooling efficiency and to avoid overstraining components. Vacuum the unit's front often. Once a year, remove the cover and vacuum behind it.

How air conditioning works

An air conditioner works on the same refrigeration principle described for a dehumidifier, and incorporates similar gas-filled coils and a compressor. However, airflow within the unit is different. Individual units are divided into separate compartments within one cabinet. Room air is drawn into the cooling compartment and passed over the evaporation coils, which absorb heat before a fan returns the air to the room at a lower temperature. As moisture vapor condenses on the coils, the unit also acts as a dehumidifier, a welcome bonus in hot, humid weather. Condensed water is normally drained to the outside of the house.

Gas in the evaporation coils carries absorbed heat to the compartment facing the outside, where it is radiated from the condenser coils and blown outside by a fan.

A thermostat operates a valve, which reverses the flow of refrigerant when the temperature in the room drops below the setting. The system is automatic so that the unit can heat the room if it is cold in the early morning. As the sun rises and boosts the temperature, the air conditioner switches over to maintain a constant temperature indoors.

Choose a unit with variable fan speed and a method for directing the chilled air where it will be most effective in cooling the whole room. Usually this is at ceiling level, where the cold air falls slowly over the whole room.

Mounting the unit

Cut a hole through the wall and fit a wood lining as described earlier for a heat-recovery ventilator. Being larger and heavier, an air conditioner needs a supporting cage or metal brackets. Units designed for installing in windows come with adjustable frames and weather stripping. After attaching the frame to the window opening, lift the air conditioner into the window, then slide it into place.

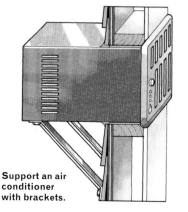

Support an air conditioner with brackets.

To reduce the running costs of an air conditioner, try to match its capacity—the amount of heat it can absorb—to the size of the room it will be cooling. A unit that is too small will be running most of the time without complete success, while one that is much too large will chill the air so quickly that it won't be able to remove much moisture vapor, and the atmosphere may still feel uncomfortable because it is humid. Ideally, the unit should only be working all the time on the hottest days.

The capacity of an air conditioner is measured in British Thermal Units (BTU). A unit with a capacity of 9000 BTU will remove that amount of heat every hour. As a rough guide to capacity, find the volume of the area you wish to cool (length x width x height), then allow 5 BTU per cubic foot. Ask the supplier to provide a more accurate calculation, which includes the size and number of windows, insulation, and heat-generating equipment in the room.

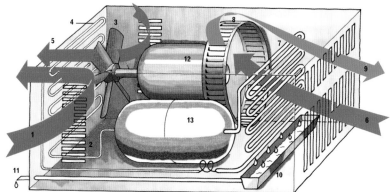

How an air conditioner works
The diagram shows the mechanism of a small wall-mounted or window-mounted air conditioner, but it illustrates the principle employed by all air conditioners. Outside air **(1)** is drawn through the side vents **(2)** by a fan **(3)** which blows it over the hot coils **(4)**. The air extracts heat from the coils and takes it outside **(5)**. Warm, humid air from the interior **(6)** is drawn over the cold coils **(7)** by a centrifugal fan **(8)** and returned to the room cooled and dry **(9)**. The condensed water drips into a reservoir **(10)** and drains to the outside **(11)**. The motor **(12)** powers the fans and the compressor **(13)**, which pumps gas around the system.

Building codes and permits

Building codes

Building codes are comprehensive guidelines intended to set standards for construction practices and material specifications. Their purpose is to ensure the adequate structural and mechanical performance, fire safety, and overall quality of buildings. They are also designed to address various health and environmental concerns related to how buildings are constructed. By setting minimum standards, building codes also limit unfair competitive practices between builders and between contractors.

Building codes address nearly every detail of building construction, from the acceptable recipes for concrete used in the foundation to the permissible fire rating of the roof finish material, and just about everything in between. Partly because codes attempt to be as comprehensive as possible, and also because they must address different concerns in different parts of the country, they are very detailed, complex, and lack uniformity from one region to another. A further complication is that many new building products become available each year that are not dealt with in the existing codes. Model codes, developed by four major organizations, are widely used for reference throughout the United States.

The Uniform Building Code, published by the International Conference of Building Officials, is very widely accepted. ICBO republishes the entire code every three years and comes out with revisions annually. A short form of the Uniform Building Code is available that covers buildings that are less than three stories high and have fewer than 6000 square feet of living space. This publication was designed for the convenience of most builders and remodelers.

The BOCA Basic Building Code, issued by the Building Officials and Code Administrators International is another widely used code. This code also comes in abridged form for residential construction.

A third model code, prepared by the American Insurance Association, and known as the National Building Code, serves as the basis for many codes that are adopted by local communities. It too is available in short form for matters relating only to home construction.

The Standard Building Code is published by the Southern Building Code Congress International. It addresses conditions and problems that are prevalent in the southern United States.

While it's likely that one of these model codes serves as the basis for the building code in your community, municipal and state governments frequently add standards and restrictions that are not in the model codes. It is your local building department that ultimately decides what is acceptable and what is not. Consult your building department for questions about any code issues. And keep in mind that building codes are primarily designed for the safety of the building's occupants and the general welfare of the community at large. It makes sense to follow all the practices outlined by the code in your area.

Building Permits

A building permit is generally required for new construction, remodeling projects that require structural changes or additions, and major demolition projects. In some areas, it's necessary to obtain a building permit for constructing an in-ground pool. In others, you even need a permit to erect scaffolding for painting your house.

To get a building permit, you must file an application (provided by your local building department) that answers questions about the proposed site and the project you are planning. You also have to file a complete set of drawings for the entire project along with detailed specifications for all the mechanical systems. A complete set normally includes a site plan, foundation plan, a plan for each floor of the house, section views of the house framing from the ridge to the foundation, elevation drawings of all four sides of the house, and drawings for all the mechanical systems. Permit fees are usually based on some percentage of the construction costs, or the numbers of trips that the inspector is likely to make to the job site, or both.

At the time you apply for a building permit, ask about other permits that may be required. For example, you may need to apply to the local health department for projects that have an impact on sewage facilities or water supply systems. It's important to arrange inspections in a timely fashion, since each ensuing stage cannot proceed until the previous work has been inspected and approved.

Anyone can file for a building permit, but if you've hired an architect or builder to handle the construction management for you, they should file for all necessary permits.

Building codes and permits

Type of work	Permit required?		Zoning approval required?	
Interior and exterior painting and minor repairs	NO	Permit may be required to erect scaffolding	NO	Unless in historic district.
Replacing windows and doors	NO		NO	Unless in historic district.
Electrical work	YES	Must be inspected	NO	Some outdoor lighting may be subject to approval.
Plumbing	YES		NO	Work involving water supply or sewage system amy require health department approval.
Heating	NO		NO	
Constructing patios and decks, Installing a hot tub	NO		NO	
Structural alterations	YES		NO	Unless house is in an historic district
Attic conversion	NO / YES	No, if work is minor like adding a simple bedroom. Yes, if major structural work is done and if plumbing and major electrical modifications are called for.	NO	Unless work impacts exterior of house in historic district
Building a fence or garden wall	NO		YES	In cases where a fence or wall is adjacent to public road, there may be height restrictions.
Planting a hedge	NO	Unless it obscures the view of traffic at a junction, or access to a main road.	NO	
Path or sidewalk	NO	Unless it will be used by the public.	NO	Unless in historic district.
Clearing land	NO		YES	
Installing a satellite-TV dish	NO		NO	
Constructing a small outbuilding	YES	Local codes usually have size restrictions. Anything smaller doesn't need a permit.	NO	Unless in historic district.
Porch addition	YES	Local codes sometimes have size limits. Under the limit doesn't require permit.	NO	Unless in historic district.
Greenhouse or sunspace	YES		NO	Unless in historic district.
Building a garage	YES		YES	If used for a commercial vehicle or located close to property line.
Driveway paving	NO		YES	At point where it meets the road.
House addition	YES		NO	Unless house is in historic district or addition will be close to property line.
Demolition	YES	If major work is done that involves any structural elements.	NO	Unless house is in historic district.
Converting single-family house into apartments	YES		YES	
Converting residential building to commercial use	YES		YES	

CHART
Building code requirements and zoning regulations vary from town to town and frequently have county and state restrictions added to them. For this reason, it's impossible to state with certainty which home-improvement projects require official permission and which do not. This chart lists some of the most frequently undertaken projects and is meant to serve as a rough guide only. Taken as a whole, it suggests a certain logic for anticipating what type of approval may be needed. Whether or not official approval is required, all work should be carried out to the standards established in local codes.

Builder's tools

BUILDER'S TOOLS

A specialist builder—such as a plasterer, finish carpenter, or bricklayer—needs only a limited set of tools, whereas the amateur is more like a one-man general builder who has to be able to tackle all kinds of construction and repair work, and therefore requires a much wider range of tools than the specialist.

The selection suggested here is for renovating and improving the structure of your home and for such tasks as building or restoring garden structures and laying paving. Electrical work, decorating, and plumbing call for other sets of tools.

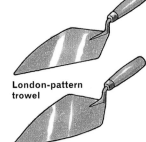

Using a mortar hawk
A mortar hawk makes tuckpointing mortar joints very easy. Place the lip of the hawk just under a horizontal joint and scrape the mortar into place with a jointer or pointing trowel.

● **Essential tools**
Brick trowel
Pointing trowel
Plasterer's trowel
Mortarboard
Hawk
Spirit level
Try square
Plumb line

FLOATS AND TROWELS

For a professional builder, floats and trowels have their specific uses, but in home maintenance a repointing trowel may often be the ideal tool for patching small areas of plaster, or a plasterer's trowel for smoothing concrete.

London-pattern trowel

Canadian-pattern trowel

Brick and block trowels

A brick or block trowel is for handling and placing mortar when laying bricks or concrete blocks. A professional might use one with a blade as long as 1 foot, but such a trowel is too heavy and unwieldy for the amateur.

The blade of a **London-pattern trowel** has one curved edge for cutting bricks, a skill that takes practice to perfect; the blade's other edge is straight, for picking up mortar. You can buy left-handed versions of this trowel or opt for a similar trowel with two straight edges.

A **Canadian-pattern trowel** (sometimes called a Philadelphia brick trowel) is also symmetrical, having a wide blade with two curved edges.

Pointing trowel

A pointing trowel is designed for repairing and shaping mortar joints between bricks. The blade is only 3 to 4 inches long.

Jointer

Use a jointer to shape the mortar joints between bricks. Its narrow blade is dragged along the mortar joint, and the curved front end is used for shaping the verticals.

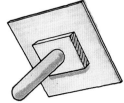

Wooden float

A wooden float is for applying and smoothing concrete to a fine, attractive texture. The more expensive ones have detachable handles, so their wooden blades can be replaced when they wear out. Similar floats made from plastic are also available.

Plasterer's trowel

A plasterer's trowel is a steel float for applying plaster and cement renderings to walls. It is also dampened and used for "polishing"—smoothing the surface of the material when it has firmed up. Some builders prefer to apply stucco with a heavy trowel and finish it with a more flexible blade, but you need to be quite skilled to exploit such subtle differences.

BOARDS FOR CARRYING MORTAR OR PLASTER

Any conveniently sized sheet of ½- or ¾-inch exterior-grade plywood can be used as a mixing board for plaster or mortar. A panel about 3 feet square makes an ideal mixing board, while a smaller board, about 2 feet square, is convenient for carrying the material to the worksite. Screwing battens to the under-side of either board makes it easier to lift and carry.

You will also need a small lightweight hawk for carrying pointing mortar or plaster. Make one by nailing a block of wood underneath a plywood board so that you can plug a handle into it.

A homemade hawk

LEVELING AND MEASURING TOOLS

You can make some leveling and measuring tools yourself—but don't skimp on essentials, such as a good spirit level and a robust tape measure.

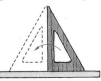

VIAL

Spirit level

A spirit level is a machine-made straight edge incorporating special glass tubes or vials that contain a liquid. In each vial an air bubble floats. When a bubble rests exactly between two lines marked on the glass, that indicates that the structure on which the level is held is precisely horizontal or vertical, depending on the orientation of the vial.

Buy a wooden or lightweight aluminum level, 2 to 3 feet long. A well-made one is very strong, but treat it with care and always clean mortar or plaster from it before it sets.

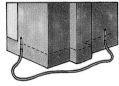

Water level

You can make a water level by plugging short lengths of transparent plastic tubing into the two ends of a garden hose; fill the hose with water until it appears in both tubes. Since water level remains constant, the levels in the tubes are always identical and so can be used for marking identical heights, even over long distances and round obstacles and bends.

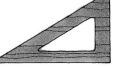

Builder's square

A large square is useful when setting out brick or concrete-block corners. The best squares are stamped out of sheetmetal, but you can make a serviceable one by cutting out a right-angle triangle from thick plywood with a hypotenuse of about 2 feet 6 inches. Cut out the center of the triangle to reduce the weight.

Checking a square

Accuracy is important, so check the square by placing it against a perfectly straight board on the floor. Draw a line against the square to make a right angle with the board, then flop the square to see if it forms the same angle from the other side.

Try square

Use a try square for marking out square cuts or joints on lumber.

Making a plumb line

Any small, heavy weight hung on a length of fine string can act as a plumb line for judging whether a structure or surface is vertical.

75

Builder's tools

Bricklayer's line

This is a nylon line used as a guide for laying bricks or blocks level. It is stretched between two flat-bladed pins, which are driven into vertical joints at the ends of a wall or between line blocks that hook over the bricks at the ends of a course. As a substitute, you can stretch string between two stakes driven into the ground outside the line of the wall.

Steel pins and line

You can buy special flat-bladed pins to hold a line that guides in laying a straight course of bricks.

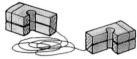

Line blocks

The blocks grip the corners of the bricks or blocks at the end of a course; the line passes through their slots.

Straightedge

Any length of straight rigid lumber can be used to check whether a surface is flat or, in conjunction with a spirit level, to see whether two points are at the same height.

Story pole

For gauging the height of brick courses, calibrate a softwood batten by making saw cuts across it at intervals equal to the thickness of a brick plus one mortar joint. Blocks of wood at each end enable a story pole to span irregularities.

Tape measure

An ordinary retractable steel tape measure is adequate for most purposes; but if you need to measure a large plot, buy a wind-up tape, 50 to 100 feet in length.

Marking gauge

A marking gauge has a sharp steel point for scoring a line on lumber parallel to the edge. It has an adjustable fence that keeps the point a constant distance from the edge.

HAMMERS

Several types of hammer are useful on a building site.

Claw hammer

Choose a strong claw hammer for building stud walls, nailing floorboards, making doorframes and window frames, and putting up garden fencing.

Hand sledge

A heavy hand sledge is used for driving cold chisels and for a variety of demolition jobs. It is also useful for driving large masonry nails into walls.

Sledgehammer

Buy a sledgehammer if you have to break up concrete or masonry. It's also the best tool for driving stakes or fence posts into the ground, though you can make do with a hand sledge if the ground is not too hard.

Mallet

A wooden carpenter's mallet is the proper tool for driving a wood chisel. But you can use a metal hammer instead if the chisel has an impact-resistant plastic handle.

SAWS

Every builder needs a range of handsaws, but consider buying a circular saw when you have to cut a lot of heavy structural lumber—especially if you have a lot of ripping to do, which is a very tiring job when done by hand.

Special saws are available for cutting metal and even for sawing through masonry.

Panel saw

All kinds of manufactured panels are used in house construction, so it is worth investing in a good panel saw.

It can also be used for cutting large structural lumber to the required lengths.

General-purpose saw

A single handsaw that can be used equally well for ripping solid planks lengthwise and crosscutting them to size is a useful tool to have on a building site. A saw with hardened teeth is also an asset.

Backsaw

This is a good saw for accurately cutting small pieces of trim, paneling, and joints. The metal stiffening along the top of the blade keeps it rigid and prevents the saw from wandering off line.

Keyhole saw

This small saw has a narrow tapered blade for cutting holes in lumber and panel stock.

Coping saw

A coping saw has a frame that holds a fairly coarse but very narrow blade under tension for cutting curves in wood.

Floorboard saw

If you pry a floorboard above its neighbors, you can cut across it with an ordinary tenon saw, but the curved cutting edge of a floorboard saw makes it easier to avoid damaging the boards on either side.

Hacksaw

The hardened-steel blades of a hacksaw have fine teeth for cutting metal. Use one to cut steel concrete-reinforcing rods or small pieces of sheetmetal.

All-purpose saw

An all-purpose saw is able to cut wood, metal, plastics, and building boards. The short frameless blade has a low-friction coating.

This type of saw is especially useful for cutting scrap lumber, which may contain nails or screws that would dull the blade of an ordinary saw.

Power jigsaw

Use a jigsaw to cut curves in wood or metal. It is also handy for cutting holes in fixed wall panels and for sawing through floorboards. A cordless saw is useful for small jobs.

Circular saw

A circular saw will quickly and accurately rip lumber or manufactured panels down to size. As well as saving you the effort of handsawing large stock, a sharp power saw produces such a clean cut that there is often no need for planing afterwards. If your preference is for a cordless circular saw, buy a spare battery and keep it charged.

Reciprocating saw

A reciprocating saw is a two-handed power saw that has a long pointed blade. It is powerful enough to saw sections of heavy lumber, and can even cut through a complete stud wall. With a change of blade, you can use a reciprocating saw to cut metal pipes. Both cordless and corded versions are available.

Gas-engine masonry saw

A gas-engine masonry saw is strictly a rental item. Still, there is no substitute for one when it comes to masonry demolition.

DRILLS

A powerful electric drill is invaluable to a builder. A cordless version is useful when you have to bore holes outdoors or in attics and cellars that lack convenient electrical outlets.

Power drill

Buy a good-quality power drill, plus a range of twist drills and spade or power-bore bits for drilling wood. Make sure the drill has a percussion or hammer action for drilling masonry walls. For masonry you need special drill bits tipped with tungsten carbide. The smaller ones are matched to the size of standard wall plugs; there are also much larger ones that have reduced shanks, so they can be used in a standard drill chuck.

Brace

A brace is the ideal hand tool for drilling large holes in lumber. In addition, when fitted with a screwdriver bit, it provides the necessary power for driving or removing large woodscrews.

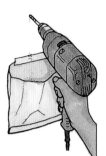

Drilling masonry for wall plugs
Set the drill to hammer action and low speed. Wrap tape around the bit to mark the depth to be drilled, allowing for slightly more depth than the length of the plug, as dust will pack down into the hole as the plug is inserted. Drill the hole in stages, partly withdrawing the bit at times to clear the debris.

To protect paintwork and floor coverings from falling dust, tape a paper bag just below the position of the hole before drilling.

● **Essential tools**
Straightedge
Tape measure
Claw hammer
Hand sledge
Panel saw
Tenon saw
Hacksaw
Keyhole saw
Power jigsaw
Power drill
Masonry bits
Brace and bits

Builder's tools

Crowbar
A crowbar, or wrecking bar, is used for demolishing lumber framework. Force the flat tip between the components and use the leverage of the long shaft to pry them apart. Choose a crowbar that has a claw at one end for removing large nails.

Slater's ripper
To replace individual slates or wooden shingles you must cut their fixing nails without disturbing the pieces overlapping them, and for this you need a slater's ripper. Pass the long hooked blade up between the shingles, locate one of the hooks over the fixing nail, and pull down sharply to cut it.

● Essential tools
Glass cutter
Putty knife
Cold chisel
Brick chisel
Spade
Shovel
Rake
Wheelbarrow
Cabinet screwdriver
Phillips-head
 screwdriver
Jack plane

GLAZIER'S TOOLS
Glass is such a hard and brittle material that it can only be worked with specialized tools.

Glass cutter
A glass cutter does not actually cut glass but merely scores a line in it. This is done by a tiny hardened-steel wheel or a chip of industrial diamond mounted in a penlike holder. The glass breaks along the scored line when pressure is applied to it.

Beam-compass cutter
A beam-compass cutter is for scoring circles on glass that enable you to either cut a round hole or create a circular pane. The cutting wheel is mounted at the end of an adjustable beam that turns on a central pivot that's attached to the glass by a suction cup.

Spear-point glass drill
A glass drill has a flat tungsten-steel tip shaped like a spearhead. The shape of the tip is designed to reduce friction that would otherwise crack the glass, but it does need lubricating with oil or water during drilling.

Hacking knife
A hacking knife is often a shop-made tool with a heavy steel blade for chipping old putty out of window rabbets in order to remove the glass. To use it, place the point between the putty and the frame, then tap the back of the blade with a hammer.

Putty knife

Putty knife
The blade of a putty knife is used for shaping and smoothing fresh putty when reglazing a window.
You can choose between a chisel type with a thick, stiff blade, or a standard putty knife with a thin, flexible blade. Putty knives are also useful for removing paint and other light-duty scraping jobs.

CHISELS
As well as chisels for cutting and paring wood joints, you'll need some special ones when you are working on masonry.

Cold chisel
Cold chisels are made from solid-steel-hexagonal-section rod. They are primarily for cutting metal bars and chopping the heads off rivets, but a builder will use one for cutting a notch in brickwork or for chopping hardware embedded in brick.
 Slip a plastic safety sleeve over the chisel to protect your hand from a misplaced blow with a hammer.

Plugging chisel
A plugging chisel has a narrow, flat tip for cutting out old or eroded pointing. It's worth having when you have a large area of brickwork to repoint.

Brick chisel
The wide blade of a brick chisel is designed for cutting bricks and concrete blocks. It is also useful for other heavy chopping and prying jobs.

WORK GLOVES
Wear strong work gloves whenever you are carrying paving rubble, concrete blocks, or rough lumber. Ordinary gardening gloves are better than none, but they won't last very long on a building site. The best work gloves have leather palms and fingers, although you may prefer a pair with ventilated backs for comfort in hot weather.

DIGGING TOOLS
Much building work requires some kind of digging—for making footing trenches and holes for concrete pads, sinking rows of postholes, and so on. You probably have the basic tools in your garden shed; the others you can rent.

Pickax
Use a medium-weight pickax to break up heavily compacted soil—especially if it contains a lot of buried rubble.

Mattock
The wide blade of a mattock is ideal for breaking up heavy clay soil, and it's better than an ordinary pickax for ground that's riddled with tree roots.

Spade
Buy a good-quality spade for excavating soil and mixing concrete. One with a stainless-steel blade is best, but alloy steel lasts reasonably well. Choose a strong hardwood or reinforced fiberglass shaft with a D-shaped handle that's riveted with metal plates on its crosspiece. Make sure the hollow shaft socket and blade are forged in one piece.
 Although square spade blades seem to be more popular, many builders prefer a round-mouth spade with a long pole handle for digging deep holes and trenches.

Shovel
You can use a spade for mixing and placing concrete or mortar, but the raised edges of a shovel retain it better.

Garden rake
Use an ordinary garden rake for spreading gravel or leveling wet concrete. Be sure to wash your rake before concrete sets on it.

Posthole auger
Rent a posthole auger to dig narrow holes for fence- and gateposts. You drive it into the ground like a corkscrew, then pull out the plugs of earth.

Wheelbarrow
Most garden wheelbarrows are not strong enough for construction, which generally involves carting heavy loads of rubble and wet concrete. Unless the tubular underframe of the wheelbarrow is rigidly braced, the wheelbarrow's thin metal body will distort and may well spill its load as you are crossing rough ground.
 Check, too, that the axle is fastened securely—a cheap wheelbarrow can lose its wheel as you are tipping a load into place.

SCREWDRIVERS
Most people gradually acquire an assortment of screwdrivers over a period of time, as and when the need arises. Alternatively, buy a power screwdriver with a range of bits or buy screwdriver bits for your power drill.

Cabinet screwdriver
Buy at least one large flat-tip screwdriver. The fixed variety is quite adequate, but a pump-action one, which drives large screws very quickly, is useful when assembling large projects.

Phillips-head screwdriver
Choose the size and type of Phillips-head screwdriver to suit the work at hand. There is no "most-useful size," as each driver must fit a screw slot exactly.

PLANES
Furniture building may call for molding or grooving planes, but most household joinery needs only a light pass to remove saw marks and leave a fairly smooth finish.

Jack plane
A jack plane, which is a medium-size bench plane, is the most versatile general-purpose tool.

77

Glossary

A

Aggregate
Particles of sand or stone mixed with cement and water to make concrete, or mortar, or added to paint for a textured finish.

B

Batt
A flat, insulating filler, as of fiberglass or mineral fiber.

Builder's sand
A fine, filtered sand used in cement or mortar mixes.

BTU
British Thermal Units. The amount of energy required to raise the temperature of one pound of water by 1 degree Fahrenheit. Used as an energy-rating guide to air conditioners and other appliances.

C

Came, cames
The grooved lead rod or rods that hold the glass in a stained-glass window.

Casing
The wooden molding around a door or window opening.

Caulk
A paste material used to seal seams and joints for weather or moisture protection. Also, to seal such joints by applying caulk.

Cavity wall
A wall of two separate masonry skins with an air space between them.

Course
A continuous layer of bricks, masonry, tiles, or other wallcovering.

D

Damp-proof course (DPC)
A layer of impervious material that prevents moisture from rising through the ground into the walls of a masonry building.

Draftproof
To make a structure impervious to drafts through insulation and construction.

Drip groove
A groove cut or molded in the underside of a door or windowsill to prevent rainwater from running back to the wall.

E

Eaves
The lower edge of a sloping roof that project beyond the walls.

Efflorescence
A white, powdery deposit caused by soluble salts migrating to the surface of masonry.

F

Fascia board
Strip of wood which covers the ends of rafters and to which gutters are attached.

Flashing
A weatherproof junction between a roof and a wall or chimney, or between one roof and another.

G

Gable roof
Two sloping roofs joined at a center ridge, forming a triangular shape.

Gambrel roof
A roof with the slope broken into two different pitches, generally one at a sharper and one at a shallower angle.

Galvanized
Covered with a protective coating of zinc.

Glazing
Architectural glasswork, glass windows, or doors.

H

Header
The top horizontal member of a wooden frame.

Hip roof
A roof with four sides, all sloping up to the center.

I

Insulation
Materials used to reduce the transmission of heat or sound. Also, nonconductive material surrounding electrical wires or connections to prevent the passage of electricity.

J

Jalousie
A window with horizontal glass louvers that adjust to allow airflow.

Jamb
A vertical upright that forms the side of an opening, or the framework of the opening as a whole.

Joist
A horizontal wooden beam used to support a floor or ceiling.

K

K-value
A measurement of heat-conducting properties, used in the construction industry to rate the insulation capability of building materials.

M

Mineral wool
A fibrous, insulating fabric.

Mullion
A thin, vertical divider between panes of a window or door.

Muntin
A central vertical member of a panel door.

P

Pointing
To form the mortar joints binding bricks together.

Polyethylene
A moisture-resistant, lightweight plastic.

Polyurethane
A polymer used in rigid foams and in various protective coatings.

Purlin
A horizontal beam that provides intermediate support for rafters or sheet roofing.

R

Rafter
One of a set of parallel sloping beams that form the main structural element of a roof.

Rock wool
A mineral fiber material used for insulation.

R-value
A measurement of a substance's ability to impede thermal passage, and so, its heat insulating quality.

S

Sash
The framework holding the panes of the window, also, the whole operable part of the window.

Sill
The lowest horizontal member of a stud partition. Also, the lowest horizontal member of a door or window frame.

Soffits
The underside of a part of a building such as the eaves, or archway.

Spalling
Flaking of the outer face of masonry caused by expanding moisture in icy conditions.

Stile
A vertical side member of a door or window sash.

Stucco
A thin layer of cement-based mortar applied to walls to provide a protective or decorative finish. Also, to apply the mortar.

T

Thermostat
A temperature-regulating mechanism.

Truss
A rigid framework, and the members thereof, forming a support structure.

U

U-value
A measurement of insulating properties.

V

Vapor barrier
A layer of impervious material which prevents the passage of moisture-laden air.

VOC
Volatile organic compound.

W

Wall plate
A horizontal member placed along the top of a wall to support the ends of joists and spread their load.

Weather strip
Thin strips of various materials set around structural openings to keep out the weather.